# 1,000,000 Books

are available to read at

# Forgotten Books

www.ForgottenBooks.com

Read online
Download PDF
Purchase in print

# 1 MONTH OF FREE READING

at

www.ForgottenBooks.com

---

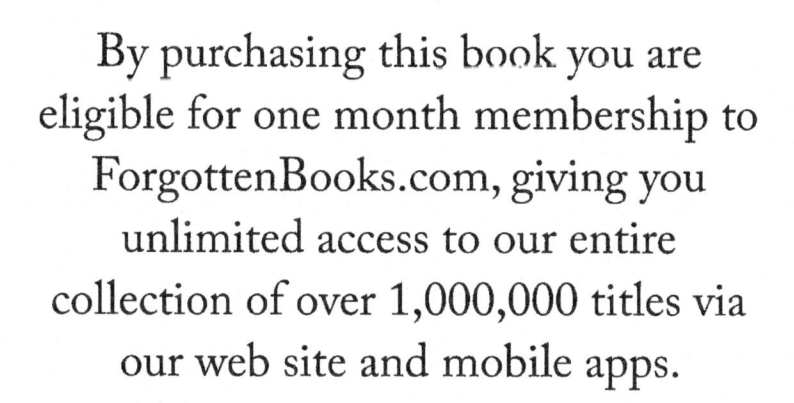

By purchasing this book you are eligible for one month membership to ForgottenBooks.com, giving you unlimited access to our entire collection of over 1,000,000 titles via our web site and mobile apps.

To claim your free month visit:
www.forgottenbooks.com/free688210

\* Offer is valid for 45 days from date of purchase. Terms and conditions apply.

English
Français
Deutsche
Italiano
Español
Português

# www.forgottenbooks.com

**Mythology** Photography **Fiction**
Fishing Christianity **Art** Cooking
Essays Buddhism Freemasonry
Medicine **Biology** Music **Ancient Egypt** Evolution Carpentry Physics
Dance Geology **Mathematics** Fitness
Shakespeare **Folklore** Yoga Marketing
**Confidence** Immortality Biographies
Poetry **Psychology** Witchcraft
Electronics Chemistry History **Law**
Accounting **Philosophy** Anthropology
Alchemy Drama Quantum Mechanics
Atheism Sexual Health **Ancient History**
**Entrepreneurship** Languages Sport
Paleontology Needlework Islam
**Metaphysics** Investment Archaeology
Parenting Statistics Criminology
**Motivational**

SMITHSONIAN INSTITUTION
BUREAU OF AMERICAN ETHNOLOGY

# DICTIONARY

## OF

# AMERICAN INDIANS

### NORTH OF MEXICO

A DESCRIPTIVE LIST OF INDIAN STOCKS, CONFEDERACIES, TRIBES, SUB-TRIBES, CLANS, GENTES, AND GEOGRAPHICAL NAMES, ACCOMPANIED BY A LIST OF THE VARIOUS NAMES BY WHICH THE INDIANS AND THEIR SETTLEMENTS HAVE BEEN KNOWN, TOGETHER WITH BIOGRAPHIES OF INDIANS OF NOTE, SKETCHES OF THEIR MANNERS AND CUSTOMS, AND A LIST OF INDIAN WORDS INCORPORATED INTO THE ENGLISH LANGUAGE.

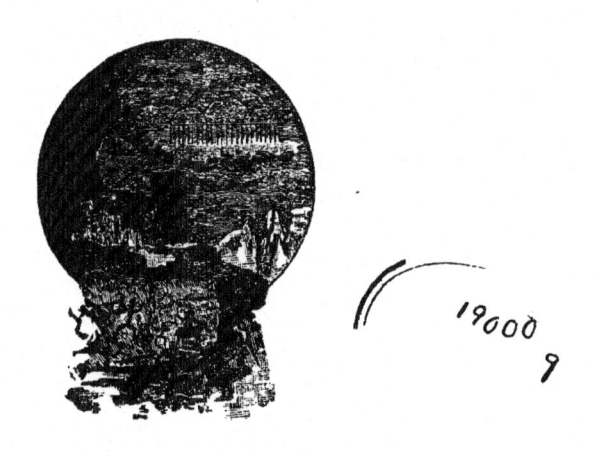

WASHINGTON

1903

SMITHSONIAN INSTITUTION
U.S. BUREAU OF AMERICAN ETHNOLOGY. Misc. Pub. #6

E
77
U53
1903
CR[55]

# DICTIONARY
## OF
# AMERICAN INDIANS

### NORTH OF MEXICO

A DESCRIPTIVE LIST OF INDIAN STOCKS, CONFEDERACIES, TRIBES, SUB-TRIBES, CLANS, GENTES, AND GEOGRAPHICAL NAMES, ACCOMPANIED BY A LIST OF THE VARIOUS NAMES BY WHICH THE INDIANS AND THEIR SETTLEMENTS HAVE BEEN KNOWN, TOGETHER WITH BIOGRAPHIES OF INDIANS OF NOTE, SKETCHES OF THEIR MANNERS AND CUSTOMS, AND A LIST OF INDIAN WORDS INCORPORATED INTO THE ENGLISH LANGUAGE.

WASHINGTON

1903

# INTRODUCTION

IN 1879 the investigations of the present Bureau of American Ethnology were begun, under the immediate direction of the late Major J. W. Powell.[1] It was understood that a study of the languages, habits, and customs of the Indian tribes inhabiting the northern portion of this continent, and especially the territories of the United States, might be made of great utility to Congress in providing the means of wise legislation for these tribes. It was understood also that it might be made of equal value to ethnological science, and Major Powell, who had passed a very considerable part of his life among these Indians, and in immediate personal contact with them, and who knew their languages and their customs at first hand, as perhaps no other trained scientific observer did, was placed in charge of the work, which was carried out in relation to every branch of ethnological investigation, on a scale which promised in time to furnish an exhaustive record of the languages, customs, arts, and location of every tribe of the great number which were the wards of Congress. The work grew as it proceeded, until, in the twenty-five volumes published or in course of publication, it came to present the greatest body of knowledge of this kind which has ever anywhere in any time been gathered. It concerns not only the material history of each tribe, but so much else that its very voluminousness makes it less easy to find any special thing wanted.

In view of the difficulty of finding, among the treasures of information contained in these volumes, what is immediately needed on any subject, it had long been the intention of Major Powell to produce a voluminous work to be called "A Cyclopedia of Indian Tribes," whose completion has been delayed by various causes, until the writer was led

[1] In 1879 Congress made an appropriation for a report on Ethnology, and ordered all the archives, records, and materials relating to the Indians of North America, collected by Major Powell, to be turned over to the Smithsonian Institution, that the work might be completed and prepared for publication under its direction. The then Secretary placed the administration of this Bureau in the charge of Major Powell, whom he appointed July 9, 1879. The Powell survey was placed by Congress under the direction of the Smithsonian Institution, without any solicitation on the Institution's part. It has endeavored faithfully to discharge, however, the duty imposed upon it. In 1880 the appropriations were made directly to the Secretary of the Institution, who later asked to be relieved from this personal responsibility, and since 1888 the appropriations have been made to the "Smithsonian Institution."

to consult him about the more immediate publication of a work which, it seemed to him, should, under the title of a "Dictionary of Indian Tribes," open all these treasures of information to the inquirer, in the form of a manual or handy volume, or volumes (at most two in number), which can be published now, and which is intended to present a brief summary of what is most important to Congress in the fund of knowledge recorded in the greater series of the annual reports of the Bureau or elsewhere, or in the great amount of its original material as yet unpublished, all presented in an alphabetical arrangement for ready reference.

Congress may find here in brief what is most important of everything that interests a legislator: an article, for example, on "Treaties," giving all that the succinctness of the Dictionary admits about treaties, with a reference to the original information in the annual volumes, where it will be found at greater length.

Again, among the first considerations of the ethnologist is the one as to the different stocks or families to which different or related tribes belong, and these families, it is found, are far better definable by their languages than by any other single consideration. It is a most notable fact that there is a greater distinction among the languages of many of our Indian tribes than among the different nations of Europe. They are not dialects of a common language, but they differ from each other as Latin and Greek, or Russian and Spanish, and these languages represent as many radical differences of habit, religion, etc. The linguistics of the tribes, then, form a starting-point of any classification which distinguishes the different physical and geographical conditions, manners, customs, laws, and religions.

An unfortunate delay, connected with the late Major Powell's failing health, has occurred in the preparation of this proposed Dictionary, but the accompanying advance pages are intended to show the scope and kind of work which is now being carried on and which it is expected will be published during the present calendar year. Incidentally I hope this work may serve as an added memorial to one who gave his life to a great work and earned by his devotion to it the trust of Congress.

S. P. LANGLEY,
*Secretary, Smithsonian Institution.*

# PREFACE

AT the time of the early exploration and settlement of North America, there were encountered many Indian tribes varying in customs and speaking a diversity of languages. Lack of knowledge of the aborigines and total ignorance of their languages led to many curious errors on the part of the early explorers and settlers: names were applied to the Indians that had no relation whatever to those by which they were aboriginally known; sometimes nicknames were bestowed, owing perhaps to some personal characteristic, fancied or real; sometimes there was applied the name given by another tribe, which was often opprobrious; frequently an effort was made to employ the designation by which a tribal group knew itself; and as such names are oftentimes unpronounceable by an alien tongue and unrepresentable by a civilized alphabet, the result was a sorry corruption, varying as the sounds were impressed on Spanish, English, French, Dutch, Russian, or Swedish ears, or were recorded in as many languages only to be as grossly corrupted when the next traveler appeared. Sometimes, again, bands of a single tribe would be given distinctive names, while clans or gentes would be regarded as independent autonomous groups to which separate tribal designations were likewise applied. Consequently, in the literature of the American Indians, which is practically co-extensive with the literature of the first three centuries of the New World, thousands of tribal names are encountered, only a small proportion of which are recognizable at a glance.

The need of a comprehensive work by means of which these names might be identified has been felt ever since a scientific interest in the Indians was first aroused. Many lists of tribes have been published, but the scientific student, as well as the general reader, until the present time, has been practically without the means of knowing any more about a given confederacy, tribe, clan, or settlement of Indians than was to be gleaned from a single casual reference to it in literature.

The present work had its inception over thirty years ago, when Prof. Otis T. Mason conceived the plan of preparing a classified list of the tribal names mentioned in the vast literature of the Indians, and in due time several thousand names were recorded on cards, with reference to the works in which they appeared. Meanwhile Mr. James Mooney began the preparation of a classified list and a series of maps showing the distribution of the tribes of the entire Western Hemisphere.

On the organization of the Bureau of American Ethnology in 1879, the work of recording the tribal synonymy was officially assigned to Professor Mason and was continued by him until other duties necessitated its suspension. Later it was placed in charge of Mr. Henry W. Henshaw, who devoted to it several years of labor, meanwhile formulating a plan to make the work encyclopedic in character and of equal importance in this respect with the synonymic feature.

Up to this time a definite classification of the tribes north of Mexico was not possible, since sufficient work of a scientific character had not been conducted toward determining their linguistic affinities. On the organization of the Bureau, however, one of the first steps taken by Major Powell was toward such a linguistic classification, and by 1885 his researches had reached a stage that warranted the grouping of the various tribes by linguistic stocks on a scientific basis. This classification is published in the Seventh Annual Report of the Bureau, and on it is based the present Dictionary.

It was at this time that Major Powell's attention was directed to the work in classification which Mr. Mooney had been conducting, and his services were thereupon enlisted by the Bureau, the entire available force of which, under Mr. Henshaw's immediate supervision, was assigned to the work that had now grown into a "Dictionary and Synonymy of the Indian Tribes North of Mexico."

As his special field Mr. Henshaw devoted attention to several of the Californian stocks and to those of the North Pacific Coast, north of Oregon, including the Eskimo. To Mr. Mooney were given the two great and historically important Algonquian and Iroquoian families, and through his wide general knowledge of the Indians he rendered aid in many directions. A list of *Linguistic Families of the Indian Tribes North of Mexico, with Provisional List of the Principal Tribal Names and Synonyms* (55 pages, octavo), prepared by Mr. Mooney, and containing about 2500 names, was at once printed for use by the collaborators of the Bureau in connection with the complete compilation, and although the list does not include the Californian tribes, it proved of great service in the earlier stages of the work.

Rev. J. Owen Dorsey assumed charge of the work on the Siouan, Caddoan, and Athapascan stocks; Dr. W. J. Hoffman, under the personal direction of Major Powell, devoted his energies to the Shoshonean family; and Mr. Jeremiah Curtin, by reason of his familiarity with the Californian tribes, rendered direct aid to Mr. Henshaw in that field. Dr. Albert S. Gatschet employed his time and long experience in the preparation of the material pertaining to the Muskhogean tribes of southeastern United States, the Yuman tribes of the Gulf of California, and various smaller linguistic groups. To Col. Garrick Mallery was assigned the French works bearing on the general subject.

## PREFACE.

With such facilities the work of compilation received a pronounced impetus, and before the close of the year named a large body of material was recorded. It should here be stated that, although the basis of the Dictionary is the literature of the Indians, many volumes of manuscript ethnologic notes and vocabularies recorded by members of the Bureau, and others, as well as a fund of general information obtained through personal study of the tribes and their languages, were utilized in its preparation.

The work was continued under Mr. Henshaw's supervision, until, in 1891, ill-health compelled his abandonment of the task. Two years previously the preparation of the material pertaining to the Yuman, Piman, Keresan, Tanoan, and Zuñian stocks of the extreme Southwest was placed in charge of Mr. F. W. Hodge, who brought it practically to completion and who meanwhile was given nominal charge of the entire work; but other official duties of members of the staff prevented the Dictionary as a whole from making much progress until some three years ago when Dr. Cyrus Thomas was entrusted with the task of bringing to date the recorded material bearing on some of the more prominent stocks.

In 1902 the work was again systematically taken up at the instance of the Secretary of the Smithsonian Institution, who detailed Mr. Hodge to undertake the general editorial supervision of the Dictionary, assisted by Mr. James Mooney, Prof. Cyrus Thomas, Mr. J. N. B. Hewitt, and Dr. John R. Swanton, of the Bureau of American Ethnology; Dr. Franz Boas, of the American Museum of Natural History; Dr. Washington Matthews, U. S. A., retired; Dr. A. L. Kroeber, of the University of California; Mr. Roland B. Dixon, of the Peabody Museum of American Archæology and Ethnology; Dr. A. F. Chamberlain, of Clark University; and Mr. Joseph D. McGuire. The material in the main was divided among these ethnologists in accordance with their special knowledge of the tribes which they had studied, and the Dictionary as now published is therefore largely the result of their labors.

Under the plan inaugurated, the scope of the Dictionary is as comprehensive as its function necessitates. It comprehends the tribes north of Mexico, with the few south of the boundary that are closely connected with those of the United States. It has been the aim to give a brief description of every linguistic stock, confederacy, tribe, subtribe or tribal division, clan, gens, and settlement known to history or even to tradition, as well as the origin and derivation of every name treated; and to record, under each, every form of the name and every other appellation by which it has been known, together with a cross-reference to each such designation.

Under the tribal descriptions a brief account of the ethnic relations of the tribe, its history (including migrations, first contact and later dealings with the white race, etc.), its location at various periods, statistics of population at different dates, etc., are included. Accompanying each synonym (the earliest known date always being given), a reference to the authority is briefly noted, and these references form a practical bibliography of the tribe for those who desire to pursue the subject further. It is not claimed that every spelling of a tribal name that occurs in print is given, but it is believed that a sufficient number of forms is recorded to enable the student to identify practically every name by which any group of Indians has been known, as well as to trace the origin of many of the terms that have been incorporated into our geographic nomenclature.

At the instance of Secretary Langley the scope of the work has recently been enlarged to include brief articles on the various customs of the Indians and of their dealings with the General Government—such as Agriculture, Fishing, Languages, Reservations, Stocks, Treaties, etc. The work includes also a representative collection of Indian geographical names, as Mississippi, Niagara, Ohio, etc., with their origin and application, as well as brief biographic sketches of Indians of note, and a list of the numerous Indian words that have been incorporated into the English language, as, for example, caucus, hickory, hominy, Mugwump, opossum, raccoon, etc.

W. H. HOLMES,
*Chief, Bureau of American Ethnology.*

# Dictionary of American Indians

**Absentee.** — The official name of a division of the Shawnee (q. v.) who, about 1845, left the rest of the tribe then in Kansas, and removed to Indian Territory. In 1901 Big Jim's band numbered 184, under a special agent, in Oklahoma; under the Sauk and Fox agency the main body numbered 503; there are also 100 Absentees and Potawatomi in Pottawatomie county. Total about 700. (J.M.)

Ginetéwi Sawanógi.—Gatschet, Shawnee MS. (B. A. E.), 1879. (So called sometimes by the other Shawnees. Ginetéwi is derived from the name of Canadian river, on which they live.)
Pépua-hapítski Sawanógi.—Ibid. (Sig.: "Away-from-here Shawnees"; commonly so called by the other Shawnees.)

**Accomac.**—The name of a tribe of the Powhatan confederacy of Virginia and also of their principal village. According to J. H. Trumbull the word means "the other-side place," or "on-the-other-side-of-water place." In the Massachuset language, *ogkomé* or *akawiné* means "beyond"; and *ac, aki,* or *ahki* in various Algonquian dialects means "land." In this sense the name has been applied to various localities. The Accomac tribe lived in Accomac and Northampton counties, east of Chesapeake bay, and according to Jefferson their principal village was about Cheriton (Cherrystone), in Northampton county. In 1608 they had 80 warriors. As they declined in numbers and importance they lost their tribal identity, and the name became applied to all the Indians east of Chesapeake bay. Up to 1812 they held their lands in common, under the name of Accomacs—living chiefly in upper Accomac county—and Gingaskins (see *Gangasco*), near Eastville, Northampton county. They were much mixed with negroes, and at the Nat Turner insurrection, about 1833, were treated as such and driven off. (J.M.)

Accawmacke.—Smith (1629), Virginia, I, 133, reprint 1819.
Accomack.—Ibid., 120.
Accowmack.—Ibid., map.
Acomack.—Ibid., II, 61.
Acomak.—Drake, Book of Indians, v, 1848.

**Achougoulas.**—Sig. probably "Pipe people," from the Choctaw *ashunga*, "pipe" (Gatschet). One of the nine villages constituting the Natchez or Nachi confederacy in 1699.—Iberville (1699) in Margry, Découvertes, IV, 179, 1880.

**Achsinnink.**—"At the rock." A village of the Unalachtigo Delawares, about 1770, on Hocking river, Ohio.—Heckewelder in Trans. Am. Philos. Soc., IV, 390, 1834.

**Acoma.**—From the native name *Akóme*, "People of the white rock," now commonly pronounced *A'-ko-ma*. The aboriginal name of their town is *A'ko*. A pueblo of the western branch of the Queres or Keresan stock, situated on a rock mesa or peñol, 357 feet in height, about 60 miles west of the Rio Grande, in Valencia county, New Mexico. Acoma is mentioned as early as 1539 by Fray Marcos de Niza, under the name *Acus*, a corruption of *Hakukia*, the Zuñi name of the pueblo; but it was first visited the following year by members of Coronado's army, who recorded the name as *Acuco*. The strength of the position of the village (which has the distinction of being the oldest inhabited settlement in the United States) is remarked by the early Spanish chroniclers, who estimated its houses at 200 and its warriors at the same number. Antonio de Espejo also visited Acoma in 1583, designating it by the name under which it is now known, attributing to it the exaggerated population of 6000, and mentioning its dizzy trail cut in the rock and its cultivated fields "two leagues away"—probably those still tilled at Acomita (Tichuna) and Pueblito (Titsiap), their two summer or farming villages 15 miles distant. Juan de Oñate, the colonizer of New Mexico, visited Acoma in 1598, when, during his governorship, Fray Andrés Corchado was assigned a mission field which included that pueblo, but no mission was actually established there at so early a date.

9

**Acoma.**—*Continued.*
The Acomas had been hostile to the surrounding village tribes during this period, and as early as 1540 are mentioned as "feared by the whole country round about." Juan de Zaldivar, of Oñate's force, visited Acoma in December, 1598, with thirty men; they were surprised by the Indians, who killed fourteen of the Spaniards outright (including Zaldivar and two other captains), and caused four others to leap over the cliff—three of whom were miraculously saved. In January, 1599, an avenging party of seventy Spaniards were despatched under Zaldivar's brother Vicente, who, after a battle which lasted three days, succeeded in killing half the tribe of about 3000 and in partly burning the town. The first missionary labor performed at Acoma was by Fray Gerónimo de Zarate-Salmeron, prior to 1629; but Fray Juan Ramirez, who went to Acoma in the spring of 1629 and remained there many years, was its first permanent missionary and the builder of the first church, which was replaced in or after 1699 by the present great structure of adobe. The Acomas participated in the general Pueblo revolt against the Spaniards in 1680 (see *Pueblo*), killing their missionary, Fray Lúcas Maldonado; but largely on account of their isolation and the inaccessibility of their village site, they were not so severely dealt with by the Spaniards as were most of the more easterly pueblos. An attempt was made to reconquer the village by Governor Vargas in August, 1696, but he succeeded only in destroying their crops and in capturing five warriors. The villagers held out until July 6, 1699, when they submitted to Governor Cubero, who changed the name of the pueblo from San Estevan de Acoma to San Pedro; but the former name was subsequently restored and is still retained. The population of Acoma dwindled from about 1500 at the beginning of the revolt to 1052 in 1760. In 1782 the mission was reduced to a *visita* of Laguna, and by the close of the century its population was only a few more than 800. Their present (1902) number is 566. The Acomas are agriculturists, cultivating by irrigation corn, wheat, melons, calabashes, etc., and raising also sheep, goats, horses, and burros. In prehistoric and early historic times they had flocks of domesticated turkeys. They are expert potters, but now do little or no weaving. The villages which they traditionally occupied after leaving Shipapu, their mythical place of origin in the north, were Kashkáchuti, Washpáshuka, Kuchtyá, Tsíama, Tapitsíama, and Katzímo or the "Enchanted mesa" (q. v.). Heáshkowa and Kowina were also pueblos occupied by Acoma clans in prehistoric times. The land grant of the tribe, made by the Spanish Government and confirmed by Congress, comprises 95,792 acres. For further information see Winship, Coronado Exped. (14th Rep. Bur Eth.); Espejo (1583) in Doc. Inéd. de Indias, xv, 100, 151; Villagran, Hist. Nueva Mexico, Alcala, 1610, repr. Mexico, 1900; Vetancurt, Crónica, and Menologia, repr. 1871; Bandelier, Hist. Introd.; ibid., Contributions; ibid., Final Report; Bancroft, Hist. Ariz. and N. M.; Lummis, Land of Poco Tiempo; Hodge, Katzimo the Enchanted, and Ascent of the Enchanted Mesa. (F.W.H.)

**Abucios.**—Duro, Don Diego de Peñalosa, 23, 1882. (= Acus of Niza.)
**Acmaat.**—Evans (1888) in Compte Rendu Cong. Int. Am., VII, 229, 1890.
**A-co.**—Bandelier in Arch. Inst. Papers, III, pt. 1, 132, 1890. (Or Aco-ma.)
**Acogiya.**—Oñate (1598) in Doc. Inéd., XVI, 102, 1871. (Doubtless the same; = Zuñi name Hakukia.)
**Acoma.**—Espejo (1583) in Doc. Inéd., xv, 116, 1871.
**Acoman.**—Hakluyt, Voyages, 469, note, 1600. (Or Acoma; quoting Espejo, 1583.)
**Acome.**—MS. of 1764 in Schoolcraft, Ind. Tribes, III, 304, 1853.
**Acomenses.**—Bancroft, Ariz. and N. Mex., 145, 1889.
**Acomeses.**—Villagran, Hist. Nueva Mexico, 158, 1610.
**Acomis.**—Taylor in Cal'a Farmer, Apr. 11, 1863.
**Acomo.**—Mota-Padilla, Hist. de la Conquista, 169, 1742.
**Acona.**—Emory, Reconnoissance, 133, 1848. (Misprint.)
**Aconia.**—Ward in Ind. Aff. Rep 1864, 191, 1865. (Misprint; *ni = m.*)
**Acquia.**—Benavides (1630) misquoted in Nouv. Ann. Voy., 5th ser., XXVII, 307, 1851.
**Acu.**—Ogilby, America, 392, 1671.
**Acuca.**—Ramusio, Nav. et Viaggi, III, 1, 1565.
**Acucans.**—Whipple in Pac. R. R. Rep., III, pt. 3, 90, 1856.
**Acuco.**—Castañeda (1540) in Winship, Coronado Exped., 519, 1896.
**Acucu.**—Coronado (1540) in Winship, Coronado Exped., 560, 1896.
**Acus.**—Niça (1539) in Hakluyt, Voy., III, 440, 1600. (Not to be confounded with Ahacus = Hawikuh.)
**Acux.**—Mota-Padilla, Hist. de la Conquista, III, 1742.
**Ago.**—Bandelier in Arch. Inst. Papers, I, 14, 1881. (Proper Queres name.)
**Ah-co.**—Lummis, Land of Poco Tiempo, 63, 1893.
**Ah-ko.**—Lummis, Man Who Married the Moon, 207, 1894.
**A'ikoka.**—Stephen in 8th Rep. B. E., 30, 1891. (Tusayan name of pueblo.)
**Aioma.**—Linschoten, Description de l'Amérique, map 1, 1638. (Misprint; *i = c.*)
**Aiomo.**—Ogilby, America, map, 1671.
**Ako.**—Loew (1875) in Wheeler Survey Rep., VII, 339, 345, 1879. (Proper name of pueblo.)

## Acoma.—Continued.

**Ako-ma.**—Bandelier in Arch. Inst. Papers, v, 173, 1890. (Tribal name.)
**Alcuco.**—Barcia, Ensayo, 21, 1723.
**Alomas.**—Mota-Padilla, Hist. de la Conquista, 515, 1742. (Probably the same, although Alona,=Halona, might have been intended.)
**A-qo.**—Bandelier in Mag. West. Hist., 668, Sept., 1886. (Proper name of pueblo.)
**Aquia.**—Jefferys, Am. Atlas, map 5, 1776. (Doubtless the same, but he locates also San Estevan de Acoma.)
**Coco.**—Alvarado (1540) in Doc. Inéd., III, 511; 1865; ibid. in Winship, Coronado Exped., 594, 1896.
**Hab-koo-kee-ah.**—Domenech, Deserts N. A., II, 53, 1860. (Misprint of Zuñi name; b = h.)
**Hacu.**—Bandelier in Mag. West. Hist., 668, Sept., 1886. (Navaho name of pueblo.)
**Hacuqua.**—Ibid., Gilded Man, 149, 1893. (Given as Zuñi name of pueblo; should be Hakukia.)
**Ha-cu-quin.**—Bandelier in Mag West Hist, 668, Sept., 1886. (Zuñi name of pueblo.)
**Hacús.**—Niça (1539) quoted by Coronado (1541) in Doc. Inéd., XIV, 322, 1870. (Same as Niça's Acus.)
**Hah-kóo-kee-ah.**—Eaton in Schoolcraft, Ind. Tribes, IV, 220, 1854. (Zuñi name of pueblo.)
**Hak-koo-kee-ah.**—Simpson in Smithson. Rep. for 1869, 333, 1871.
**Ha-ku.**—Bandelier in Arch. Inst. Papers, v, 173, 1890. (Or Ha-ku-kue. Given as Zuñi name of pueblo; really their name for the Acomas.)
**Ha-ku Kue.**—Ibid., III, pt. 1, 132, 1890; v, 169, 1890. (Improperly given as Zuñi name of pueblo.)
**Ha-kus.**—Ibid., v, 173, 1890. (Navaho name of pueblo; see Hacu, above.)
**Peñol.**—Alcedo, Dic.-Geog., IV, 140, 1788. (So named from the mesa on which it stands.)
**Quebec of the Southwest.**—Lummis, Land of Poco Tiempo, 57, 1893.
**Quéres Gibraltar.**—Ibid., 57.
**San Estéban de Acoma.**—Vetancurt, Teatro Mex., III, 319, 1871. (Mission name.)
**San Pedro.**—Bancroft, Ariz. and N. Mex., 221, 1889. (Mission name after July, 1699.)
**Suco.**—Galvano (1563) in Hakluyt Society, XXX, 227, 1862. (Misquoting Acuco of Coronado; also applied to Cicuic,= Pecos.)
**Tuthla-huay.**—Bandelier in Arch. Inst. Papers, IV, pt. 2, 235, 1892. (Tigua name.)
**Vacus.**—Niça, Relation, in Ramusio, Nav. et Viaggi, III, 357, 1565.
**Vsacus.**—Ibid.
**Yacco.**—Oñate (1598) in Doc. Inéd., XVI, 115, 1871. (Identified by Bandelier (Jour. Am. Eth. and Arch., III, 80, 1892) with Acoma; misprint of the Spanish *y Acco* = " and Acco.")
**Yaco.**—Columbus Memorial Vol., 155, 1893. (Misprint of Oñate's " Yacco.")

**Agriculture.**—An opinion long prevailed in the minds of the people that the Indians north of Mexico were, previous to and at the time Europeans began to settle that part of the continent, virtually nomads having no fixed abodes and hence practising agriculture to a very limited extent. Why this opinion has been entertained by the masses, who have learned it from tales and traditions of Indian life and warfare since the establishment of European colonies in this country, can be readily understood, but why writers, who have had access to the older records, should thus speak of them is not easily explained, when these records, speaking of the temperate regions, almost without exception notice the fact that the Indians, although addicted to war, much devoted to the chase, and often base and treacherous, were generally found, from the border of the western plains to the Atlantic, dwelling in settled villages and cultivating the soil. De Soto found all the tribes he visited, from the Florida peninsula to the western part of Arkansas, cultivating maize and various other food plants. The early voyagers along the Atlantic found the same thing true from Florida to Massachusetts. Capt. John Smith and his Jamestown colony, and indeed all the early colonies, depended at first very largely for subsistence on the products of Indian cultivation. Jacques Cartier, the first European who ascended the St. Lawrence, found the Indians of Hochelaga (now Montreal) cultivating the soil. "They have," he remarks, "good and large fields of corn . . . which they preserve in garrets at the tops of their houses." Champlain and the early French explorers testify to the large reliance of the Iroquois on the cultivation of the soil for subsistence. La Salle and his companions observed the Indians of Illinois, and thence southward along the Mississippi, cultivating and to a large extent subsisting on maize.

F. Gabriel Sagard Theodat, a witness of what he reports, says, in speaking of the agriculture of the Hurons, in 1623-26: "They lop off the branches of the trees which they have cut down and burn them at the foot of these, and in the course of time they remove the roots, and then the women thoroughly clear up the ground and dig a round place at every two feet or less, where they plant in the month of May in each one nine or ten grains of corn which they have previously selected, culled, and soaked for several days in water; and thus they continue in this manner so that they have enough provision for two or three years, either from fear that a bad year may come upon them, or rather that they may go to trade it, by exchange for peltries or other things they may need, with other nations. And every year they thus plant their corn in the same places and spots, which they renew with their small wooden shovels, the remainder of the land being uncultivated, but only cleared from noxious weeds, so that it appears that these [spaces between the rows of corn] are paths

Agriculture.—*Continued.*
[*chemins*], so careful are they to keep them clean, and this is the cause that, going alone sometimes from our village to another, I got lost ordinarily in these fields of corn, rather than in the prairies or forests" (Hist. du Canada, I, 265-66, 1636).

Maize, or Indian corn, the great American cereal, was, at the time of the discovery, in cultivation from Peru in South America to the climatic limit in North America. "It [maize] was found in cultivation from the southern extremity of Chili to the fiftieth parallel of north latitude, beyond which limits the low temperature renders it an uncertain crop" (Brinton, Myths of the New World, 23, 1876). "All the nations I have known and who inhabit from the sea as far as the Illinois, and even farther, which is a space of about 1500 miles, carefully cultivate the maize corn, which they make their principal subsistence" (Du Pratz, Hist. La., II, 239, 1763). "The whole of the tribes situated in the Mississippi valley, in Ohio, and the Lakes reaching on both sides of the Alleghanies, quite to Massachusetts and other parts of New England, cultivated Indian corn. It was the staple product" (Schoolcraft, Ind. Tribes, I, 80, 1851). It is unnecessary, however, to multiply quotations on this point, as it is universally admitted.

Beans, squashes, pumpkins, potatoes, and tobacco were also cultivated to some extent, especially in what are now the Gulf and South Atlantic states. The long time previous to the discovery during which maize had been in cultivation is proven by the fact of differentiation into varieties of the cultivated product. Hariot, writing as early as 1587 (Brief and True Report of Va., repr. 1872), mentions four different varieties. Beverley says: "Our natives had originally amongst them, Indian corn, peas, beans, potatoes [sweet potatoes] and tobacco. This Indian corn was the staff of food upon which the Indians did ever depend. . . . There are four sorts of Indian corn, two of which are early ripe, and two late ripe, all growing in the same manner. . . . The late ripe corn is diversified by the shape of the grain only, without respect to the accidental differences in colour, some being blue, some red, some yellow, some white, and some streak'd. That therefore which makes the distinction is the plumpness or shrivelling of the grain; the one looks as smooth and as full as the early ripe corn and this they call flint corn; the other has a larger grain and looks shrivell'd, with a dent on the back of the grain as if it had never come to perfection, and this they call '*she-corn*'" (Beverley, Hist. Va., 125-128, 2d ed., Lond., 1722). According to the same authority the Indians had two varieties of sweet potatoes.

Marquette, speaking of the Illinois Indians, says that in addition to maize, "they also sow beans and melons, which are excellent, especially those with a red seed. Their squashes are not of the best; they dry them in the sun to eat in the winter and spring" (Voy. and Discov., Hist. Coll. La., IV, 33, 1852).

Some idea of the extent of the cultivation of maize by some of the tribes may be gained from the following estimates: The amount of corn of the Iroquois destroyed by Denonville in 1687 was estimated at one million bushels (Charlevoix, Hist. Nouv. Fr., II, 355, 1744; also Doc. Hist. N. Y., I, 238, 1849). According to Tonty, who accompanied the expedition, they were engaged seven days in cutting up the corn of four villages. General Sullivan, in his expedition into the same country, destroyed 160,000 bushels of corn and cut down the Indian orchards; in one orchard alone fifteen hundred apple trees were destroyed (Hist. N. Y. during the Revolutionary War, II, 334, 1879). General Wayne, writing from Grand Glaize in 1794, says, "The margins of these beautiful rivers,— the Miamis of the Lake and the Au Glaize,—appear like one continuous village for a number of miles, both above and below this place; nor have I ever before beheld such immense fields of corn in any part of America from Canada to Florida" (Manypenny, Our Ind. Wards, 84, 1880).

If we are indebted to the Indians for maize, without which the peopling of America would probably have been delayed a century, it is also from them the whites learned the method of planting, storing, and using it. The cribs set on posts, so common in the South, are copies of those in use among the Indians, which Lawson (Hist. Carolina, 35, repr. 1860) so fully describes.

The foregoing applies chiefly to the region east of the Rocky mountains, but the native population of the section now embraced in New Mexico, Arizona, and California in part not only cultivated the soil, but relied

**Agriculture.**—*Continued.*
on agriculture to a large extent for subsistence. Frequent mention is made by the chroniclers of Coronado's expedition to New Mexico of the general cultivation of maize by the Indians of that section, and also of the cultivation of cotton. It is stated in the Relacion del Suceso (Winship in 14th Rep. Bur. Eth., 575), that those who lived near the river raised cotton, but the others did not. The writer, speaking of the Rio Grande valley, adds, "There is much corn here."

"From the earliest information we have of these nations [the Pueblo Indians] they are known to have been tillers of the soil, and though the implements used and their methods of cultivation were both simple and primitive, cotton, corn, wheat [after its introduction], beans, with many varieties of fruits were raised in abundance" (Bancroft, Nat. Rac., 1, 538, 1882).

The Indians of New Mexico and Arizona had learned the art of irrigating their fields before the appearance of the white man on the continent. This is shown not only by the statements of early explorers, but by the still existing remains of their ditches. "In the valleys of the Salado and Gila, in southern Arizona, however, casual observation is sufficient to demonstrate that the ancient inhabitants engaged in agriculture by artificial irrigation to a vast extent. . . . Judging from the remains of extensive ancient works of irrigation, many of which may still be seen passing through tracts cultivated today as well as across densely wooded stretches considerably beyond the present non-irrigated area, it is safe to say that the principal canals constructed and used by the ancient inhabitants of the Salado valley controlled the irrigation of at least 250,000 acres" (Hodge, Preh. Irrigation in Arizona, Am. Anthrop., July, 1893). Remains of ancient irrigating ditches and canals are also found elsewhere in this southwestern section.

How far to the north on the Pacific side the cultivation of maize had been carried in prehistoric times is not positively known, but, judging by the Indian names applied to the cereal, it is believed that the northern limit was yet south of the present northern boundary of California.

The sunflower was cultivated to a limited extent both by the Indians of the Atlantic slope and those of the Pueblo region for its seeds, which were eaten after being parched and beaten into a meal between two stones. The limits of the cultivation of tobacco at the time of the discovery has not as yet been well defined. That it was cultivated to some extent on the Atlantic side is known; that it was in use in the sixteenth century as far north on the Pacific side appears probable.

Although it has been stated that the Indians did not use fertilizer, there were exceptions to this rule. The Plymouth colonists were told by the Indians to add fish to the old grounds (Bradford's Hist. Plym. Plan., Mass. Hist. Coll., 4th ser., III, 60). It is also stated that the Iroquois manured their land. Lescarbot says the Armouchiquois, Virginiens, and others "enrich their fields with shells and fish." The implements they used in cultivating the ground are described as "wooden howes" and "spades made of hard wood." "Florida Indians dig their ground with an instrument of wood fashioned like a broad mattock," "use hoes made of shoulder blades of animals fixed on staves," "use the shoulder blade of a deer or a tortoise shell, sharpened upon a stone and fastened to a stick instead of a hoe"; "a piece of wood, three inches broad, bent at one end and fastened to a long handle sufficed them to free the land from weeds and turn it up lightly." Such are the earlier statements in regard to the agricultural implements used by the Indians; however, a certain class of stone implements has been found in great numbers, which are generally conceded to have been used in breaking the soil.

The field work was usually, though not entirely, done by the women. Hariot (Hakluyt, Voy., III, 329, 1801) says, "The women, with short pickers or parers, because they use them sitting, of a foot long, and about five inches in breadth, do only break the upper part of the ground to raise up the weeds, grass, and old stubs or corn-stalks with their roots." It was a general custom to burn over the ground before planting in order to free it from weeds and rubbish. In the forest region patches were cleared by girdling the trees, thus causing them to die, and afterward burning them down.

Though the Indians as a rule have been somewhat slow in adopting the plants and methods introduced by the whites, this has not been wholly because of their dislike of labor, but

Agriculture.—*Continued.*
has been due, largely to their frequent removals by the Government and to the unproductive quality of the soil of the reservations assigned them. Where tribes or portions of tribes, as parts of the Cherokee and Iroquois, were allowed to remain in their original territory, they were not slow in bringing into use the introduced plants and farming methods of the whites, as fruit trees, stock, plows, etc.

According to the Report of the Commissioner of Indian Affairs for 1901, the following is a summary of the agricultural industries of the Indians, exclusive of the "Five Civilized Tribes," during that year:

| | | |
|---|---|---|
| Land cultivated.....acres | | 355,261 |
| Land broken........ | " | 28,641 |
| Land under fence.... | " | 1,289,689 |
| Fencing built....... rods | | 189,975 |
| Families living on and cultivating lands in severalty | | 10,270 |

Crops raised:

| | | |
|---|---|---|
| Wheat...........bushels | | 935,870 |
| Oats and barley.. | " | 737,986 |
| Corn........... | " | 668,994 |
| Vegetables........ | " | 441,931 |
| Flax........... | " | 20,387 |
| Hay................tons | | 289,335 |

Miscellaneous products of Indian labor:

| | |
|---|---|
| Butter made.....pounds | 118,554 |
| Lumber sawed.......feet | 5,716,000 |
| Timber marketed... " | 141,850,000 |
| Wood cut....... ..cords | 91,184 |

Stock owned by Indians:

| | |
|---|---|
| Horses, mules, and burros.................... | 343,300 |
| Cattle................. | 253,819 |
| Swine................ | 50,365 |
| Sheep................ | 567,941 |
| Goats................ | 90,913 |
| Domestic fowls......... | 254,285 |
| Freight transported by Indians with their own teams......pounds | 21,857,000 |
| Amount earned by such freighting.......... | $92,770 |

Value of products of Indian labor sold by Indians:

| | |
|---|---|
| To Government........ | $436,307 |
| Otherwise...............$ | 1,049,185 |
| Roads made........miles | 264 |
| Roads repaired....... | 1,363 |

Much additional information regarding agriculture among the Indians may be found throughout the Annual Reports of the Bureau of American Ethnology. See also Food. (C.T.)

Alleghany.—This is the Delaware (Algonquian) name of the northeastern branch of upper Ohio river. It is synonymous with the term *Ohio* in both signification and application; but today its application is restricted to a branch of the river of which it was the name. It is composed of two elements, represented by *Alleg* and *hany*. The first part is the Delaware and cognate *wĕlihk*, "good, fine, beautiful"; and the latter is *hany* for *hana*, sometimes written *an*, *anna*, and *han*, signifying "river, stream of water," in the same tongue. Thus, *Alleghany*, meaning "(It is) a fine, or beautiful, river," is a literal translation of the name *Ohio* of Iroquoian origin. The Cavalier de La Salle, in 1679, in detailing the advantages the Ohio river seemed to him to have for the carrying of the western fur trade, says that it is "a river which I have found"; and, a little farther on, that it is that "which I have called the *Baudrane*. The Iroquois call it *Ohio*, and the Outaouas *Olighin-cipou*" (Margry, Découvertes, pt. I, p. 114; pt. II, pp. 79-80). But, in the Acte de Prise de Possession, dated March 13, 1682, La Salle uses the following language, namely, "from the mouth of the river Saint-Louis, called Ohio, Olighin-sipou and Chukagoua" (op. cit., pt. II, p. 184). On page 96, he writes the last name Suskakoua, which is evidently a name of Cumberland river. Now, Olighinsipou, the preferable orthography of the name, is in its first element cognate with the appellation *Alleghany;* for *Olighin* is evidently *Wĕlihk-in*, "good, fine, beautiful," the final *-in* being the sign of the so-called inanimate gender, which is unexpressed in the name *Alleghany*. The element *sipou*, or *cipou*, signifies "river, stream of water." So *Olighin-sipou* also signifies "(It is) a fine, or beautiful, river." (J.N.B.H.)

Amusements.—When not bound down by stern necessity, the Indian at home was occupied with a constant round of dancing, feasting, and gaming. While most of the dances were religious or otherwise ceremonial in character, there were others which had no other purpose than that of social pleasure. They might be in the day or the night, general or confined to particular societies, and were usually with the accompaniment of the drum, rattle, or other musical instrument to help out the song. Many dances were of pantomimic or dramatic character. The giving of presents was a constant feature of the dance, as was betting on all athletic contests

**Amusements.**—*Continued.*
and ordinary games. The games of the Eskimo and extreme northern tribes were chiefly athletic, such as racing, wrestling, throwing of heavy stones, and tossing in a blanket. From Hudson bay to the Gulf of Mexico, and from the Atlantic to the border of the plains, the great athletic game was the ball play, now adopted in civilization under the name of *la crosse*. In the north it was played with one racket, and in the south with two. Athletes were regularly trained to this game, which was frequently played as an intertribal affair. The "wheel-and-stick" game in one form or another was well-nigh universal. As played in the east one gamester rolled forward a stone disk, or wheel, while his opponent slid after it a stick carved at one end in such a way that the wheel, when it fell to the ground, would rest within the crook of the stick. On the plains a wooden wheel, frequently netted, took the place of the stone disk. Like most other Indian things, the game has a symbolic significance in connection with the sun myth. A sacred variant of the game was played by the priests for divinatory purposes. Target practice with arrows, knives, or hatchets thrown from the hand, as well as with the bow and rifle was also universal among the warriors and boys of the various tribes. The gaming arrows were of special design and ornamentation, and the game itself had often a symbolic purpose. Horse-races, frequently intertribal, were prominent amusements on the plains during the warm season; while foot-races, often elaborately ceremonial in character, were common among the sedentary agricultural tribes, particularly the Pueblos and the Wichita.

Games resembling dice and "hunt-the-button" were found everywhere, and were played by both sexes alike, particularly in the tipi, or wigwam, during the long winter nights. The dice, or equivalents, were stone, bone, fruit-seeds, shells, wood, or reed, variously shaped and marked. They were thrown from the hand or from a small basket bowl. One form, the "awl game," confined to the women alone, was played around a blanket, which had various tally marks along the border for marking the progress of the game. The "hunt-the-button" games were usually accompanied with songs and rhythmic movements of the hands and body, intended to confuse the parties whose task was to guess the location of the button. Investigations by Mr Stewart Culin show a close correspondence between these Indian games and those of China, Japan, Korea, and northern Asia.

Special women's games were shinny, football, and the "deer-foot" game, besides the awl game already noted. In football the main object was to keep the ball in the air as long as possible by kicking it upward from the toes. The "deer-foot" game was played with a number of perforated bones from a deer's foot, strung upon a beaded cord, having a needle at one end. The purpose was to toss the bones in such a way as to catch a particular one upon the end of the needle in its descent.

With the children there were target shooting, stilts, slings, and tops for the boys, and buckskin dolls and playing house for the girls. As among civilized nations, the children found the greatest delight in imitating the occupations of the elders. Numerous references to amusements among the various tribes may be found throughout the Annual Reports of the Bureau of American Ethnology. A special memoir on the "Games of the American Indians," by Mr Culin, will appear in a forthcoming report. See DANCES.  (J. M.)

**Camass, kamass, quamash.**—A small plant (*Camassia esculenta*) with edible roots growing in British Columbia and neighboring portions of the United States. The name has been adopted from the Nootka of Vancouver island, and has been applied in the Latinized form to the genus to which the above belongs. This is related to *Scilla* of the Old World. It has also been adopted as the name of several places in Montana, Idaho, and Oregon, as well as for the camass-rat (*Thomomys talpoides*) which subsists principally on the roots of this plant.  (J.R.S.)

**Cayuse.**—Originally a breed of Indian pony used by the Waiilatpu or Cayuse Indians of Oregon, from whom it receives its name; but the term is now generally applied in that section to any Indian pony.  (J.R.S.)

**Cherokee.**—Properly Tsálăkĭ' (Upper dialect) or Tsárăgĭ (Lower dialect). Adair derives this word from *atsĭlă*, or *atsĭră*, "fire," to which he says the Cherokee paid great honors. This

**Cherokee.**—*Continued.*
derivation is not possible, however, as the leading part of *atsĭlă* always remains *tsil*, never changing to *tsal;* while, as regards the latter part of his statement, they paid no greater honors to fire than to water, thunder, or any other of their chief daimons. Morgan incorrectly renders the word 'great people." A more probable derivation seems to be from *sáhălăkĭ'*, an "upland field," as distinguished from *klâkés*, a bottom field along a stream; the Cherokee being peculiarly an upland tribe, it is possible that they so designated their country in their first intercourse with the whites. The Iroquois called them Oyada-ono, or "cave people," also in allusion to the broken, mountainous nature of their country; while the Algonquian tribes generally knew them as Kittuwa, which Brinton incorrectly thinks may be derived from a Delaware term signifying "people of the great wilderness," while Heckewelder also makes it a Delaware word, probably meaning "travelers" or "wanderers," but which the Cherokee themselves say is derived from the name of one of their principal ancient settlements, Kituhwu (q. v.). The fact that the Cherokee speak an Iroquoian language points to an ancient connection with the Iroquois tribes, and all the evidence goes to show that the Cherokee are identical with the people known traditionally to the Delawares as Talligewi. According to tradition, the Talligewi, at the period when the Delawares and Iroquois first arrived in the eastern part of the United States, were a powerful people, occupying the entire valley of the Ohio and Alleghany rivers. After a long war, in the course of which they built the numerous ancient earthworks of that region for their defense, they were finally driven out by the invading Delawares and Iroquois and fled toward the south. In the *Walam Olum*, the national legend of the Delawares, there are numerous references to these Talligewi. According to this authority, they were driven southward before the separation of the Nanticoke and Shawnee from the parent Lenape, and long afterward— even subsequent to the appearance of the whites on the eastern coast— there is a notice of a war carried on by the Delawares against the Talligewi and Coweta (Creeks) in the south. In the name Talligewi, frequently written Alligewi, the final *wi* is merely the Algonquian plural ending, without which the word becomes Talligé, which strikingly resembles Tsalaki, the name which the Cherokee apply to themselves. Heckewelder, the great authority on the Delawares, was of the opinion that Talligewi was a foreign word adopted by that tribe. According to the tradition of the Cherokee as given by Haywood (Nat. and Aborig. Hist. Tenn.), they claim that "they came from the upper part of the Ohio, where they erected the mounds on Grave creek, and that they removed hither (to East Tennessee) from the country where Monticello is situated." The large mound near Monticello, Virginia, mentioned by Jefferson as well known to the southern Indians, may have some connection with this tradition. Brinton, after summing up the arguments in favor of the identity of the Cherokee with the Alligewi, concludes with these words: "Name, location and legends, therefore, combine to identify the Cherokees, or Tsalaki, with the Tallike; and this is as much evidence as we can expect to produce in such researches."

The Cherokee were formerly the leading tribe of the southern states, and are now the most advanced and prosperous in the country, and second only to the Sioux, and perhaps the Ojibwa, in population. They possessed an extensive territory centering in the southern Alleghanies and embracing the mountainous portions of southern Virginia, North Carolina, South Carolina, Georgia, Alabama, and Tennessee, and they also set up a claim to the whole of Kentucky and West Virginia. According to tradition they once lived in Virginia, and they are probably the Rickohockans or Rechahecrians mentioned by early writers as living in the mountains of that state, and who, in 1658, overran the lowlands as far as Richmond. They formerly extended farther down toward the coast on their southeastern frontier, but were driven back by the Creek tribes within the historic period. Their principal settlements were on the headwaters of Savannah and Tennessee rivers, where they are said to have had at one time sixty settlements. Those living on the Savannah were called Eratĭ Tsálăkĭ, or Lower Cherokee, while those on the waters of the Tennessee were known as Awtălĭ Tsálăkĭ, or Upper Cherokee (Otali), and spoke a different dialect. On the waters of the Tuckaseegee river, be-

**Cherokee.**—*Continued.*
tween the Upper and Lower Cherokee, were the Middle Cherokee, speaking a third dialect, forming the connecting link between the other two. This is the dialect now chiefly spoken on the East Cherokee reservation. The Upper dialect is the literary dialect, while the Lower dialect—the only one having the *r*—is now practically extinct. The Cherokee were always closely associated with the Shawnee, and at war with the Iroquois. For a long period the Shawnee lived adjacent to them in Tennessee, and in 1795 a band of Cherokee was living with the Shawnee on Scioto river in Ohio. The main body of the Shawnee are now confederated with the Cherokee in Indian Territory. As the white settlements gradually extended into the interior of Carolina the Cherokee were pressed back into the mountains, and about the period of the Revolution they began to form new settlements along the middle Tennessee and in upper Georgia and Alabama. Here they remained, with constantly contracting limits, until, by the treaty of New Echota in 1835, they sold all their remaining country and removed soon after to a new tract assigned them west of the Mississippi, being joined there by a party of the tribe which had previously settled in Arkansas.

When the main body removed in 1838, a number of individuals who had decided to abandon their tribal relations remained behind, and most of these, with a large number of fugitives who had fled to the mountains during the removal, gradually concentrated in western North Carolina, and are now known as the Eastern Band of Cherokees.

Of their fourteen clans the Wolf is the leading one, and the Wolf, Bird, Paint, and Deer clans seem to be most numerous, while some of the others are perhaps now extinct, although their names are still remembered. There were originally seven clans, the others having been formed by separation from these. The seven original clans seem to have had a connection with the "seven mother towns" of the Cherokee, described by Cumming in 1730 as having each a chief, whose office was hereditary in the female line.

The Cherokee are probably about as numerous now as at any period in their history. With the exception of an estimate in 1730 which placed them at about 20,000, most of the estimates up to a recent period give them but 12,000 or 14,000 souls, and in 1758 they were computed at only about 7500. The majority of the earlier estimates are probably too low, as the Cherokee occupied so extensive a territory that only a part of them came in contact with the whites. In 1708 Governor Johnson estimated them at sixty villages and "at least 500 men" (Rivers, South Carolina, 238, 1856). In 1715 they were officially reported to number 11,210 (Upper, 2760; Middle, 6350; Lower, 2100) souls, including 4000 warriors, and living in sixty villages (Upper 19, Middle 30, Lower 11). In 1720 they were estimated to have been reduced to about 10,000, and again in the same year reported at about 11,500 souls, including about 3800 warriors (Gov. Johnson's Report, 1720, in Rivers, Early Hist. South Carolina, 93, 94, 103, 1874). In 1729 they were estimated at 20,000 souls, at least 6000 warriors and sixty-four towns and villages (Stevens, Hist. Ga., I, 48–49, 1847). They are said to have lost a thousand warriors in 1739 from smallpox and rum, and suffered a steady decrease during their wars with the whites, extending from 1760 to the close of the Revolution. They had again increased to 16,542 at the time of their forced removal to the west in 1838, but a large number perished in the transit, 311 going down together in a steamboat collision on the Mississippi. The Civil War in 1861–65 again checked their progress, but they recovered from its effects in a remarkably short time, and in 1885 numbered about 19,000, of whom about 17,000 were in the Indian Territory, together with about 5000 whites, negroes, Delawares, and Shawnee, while the remaining 2000 were still in their ancient homes in the east. Of this "Eastern Band," 1376 are on the East Cherokee (Qualla) reservation in Swain and Jackson counties, North Carolina; about 300 more are on Cheowah river in Graham county, North Carolina; while the remainder—chiefly mixed bloods—are scattered over East Tennessee and northern Georgia and Alabama. The Eastern Band lost about 300 by smallpox at the close of the Civil War. By the census of 1898 there were in Indian Territory 26,500 persons of Cherokee blood, including all degrees of admixture. There were also 871 Delawares, 790 Shawnee, and 4000 negro freedmen living with the tribe.

**Cherokee.**—*Continued.*
The Cherokee have a large admixture of white blood.

For the Cherokee settlements, see IROQUOIAN; and for further information concerning the tribe, particularly regarding its dealings with the United States, see Royce, Cherokee Nation of Indians, Fifth Report. Bur. Eth., 121, 1887; Indian Land Cessions, Eighteenth Rep. Bur. Eth., *passim*, 1899; Mooney, Cherokee Myths, Nineteenth Report, 1900. (J.M.)

**Achalaque.**—De Soto (1539) in Garcilaso de la Vega, III, 1723; Schoolcraft, Ind. Tribes, II, 35, 1852. (Spanish name in 1540.)
**Allegans.**—Colden, map (1727) in Schoolcraft, Ind. Tribes, III, 525, 1853.
**Allegewe.**—Hind, Labrador Peninsula, II, 7, 1863.
**Allegewi.**—Schoolcraft, Ind. Tribes, V, 133, 1855.
**Allegewy.**—Ibid., II, 37, 1852.
**Alleghans.**—Hall, N. W. States, 29-31, 1849.
**Alleghanys.**—Rafinesque in Marshall, Ky., I, 34, 1824.
**Allegwi.**—Squier in Beach, Ind. Misc., 26, 1877.
**Alligewi.**—Heckewelder (1819) in Schoolcraft, Ind. Tribes, III, 525, 1853.
**Allighewis.**—Keane in Stanford, Compendium, 500, 1878.
**Callageheahs.**—McKenney and Hall, Ind. Tribes, I, 186, 1854. (Evidently the Cherokee.)
**Chalakee.**—Nuttall, Journal, 124, 1821.
**Chalaque.**—Gentleman of Elvas (1540) in Hakluyt Soc., Florida, 60, 1851.
**Chalaquies.**—Barcia, Ensayo, 335, col. 1, 1723. (Spanish name.)
**Charakees.**—Homann Heirs map, 1756.
**Charakeys.**—Ibid., about 1730.
**Charikees.**—Document of 1718 in Rivers, South Carolina, 55, 1856.
**Charokees.**—Johnson (1720) in Rivers, Early Hist. S. C., 93, 1874.
**Cheelake.**—Barton, New Views, xliv, 1798. (Given as Upper Cherokee form.)
**Cheerake.**—Adair, Am. Inds., 226, 1775.
**Cheerakee.**—Ibid., 137.
**Cheeraque's** (mountain).—Moore (1704) in Carroll, Hist. Coll. S. C., II, 576, 1836.
**Cheerokee.**—Ross (1776?) in Hist. Mag., 2d ser., II, 218, 1867.
**Chel-a-ke.**—Long, Exped. Rocky Mts., II, lxx, 1823.
**Chelakees.**—Gallatin in Trans. Am. Ant. Soc., II, 90, 1836.
**Chelaques.**—Nuttall, Journal, 247, 1821.
**Chelekee.**—Keane in Stanford, Compendium, 506, 1878.
**Chellokee.**—Schoolcraft, Ind. Tribes, II, 204, 1852.
**Cheloculgee.**—White, Statistics of Ga., 28, 1849. (Creek name; singular, Che-lo-kee.)
**Chelokees.**—Gallatin in Trans. Am. Ant. Soc., II, 104, 1836. (See White, next above.)
**Cheokees.**—Johnson (1772) in N. Y. Doc. Col. Hist., VIII, 314, 1857. (Misprint.)
**Cheraguees.**—Coxe, Carolana, II, 1741.
**Cherahes** (mountains).—Brickell (1737) in Haywood, Tenn., 224, 1823.
**Cherakees.**—Coxe, Carolana, map, 1741.
**Cherakis.**—Chauvignerie (1736) in Schoolcraft, Ind. Tribes, III, 555, 1853.
**Cheraquees.**—Coxe, Carolana, 13, 1741.
**Cheraquis.**—Pénicaut (1699) in Margry, Découvertes, V, 404, 1883.
**Cherickees.**—Clarke (1739) in N. Y. Doc. Col. Hist., VI, 148, 1855.
**Cherikee.**—Albany conference (1742) in ibid., 218.
**Cherokee.**—Johnson (1708) in Rivers, South Carolina, 238, 1856.
**Cherokis.**—Rafinesque, Am. Nations, I, 140, 1836.
**Cherookees.**—Croghan (1760) in Mass. Hist. Soc. Coll., 4th ser., IX, 372, 1871.
**Cheroquees.**—Campbell (1761) in ibid., 416.
**Cherrackees.**—Evans (1755) in Gregg, Old Cheraws, 15, 1867.
**Cherrokees.**—Treaty of 1722 in Drake, Book of Ind's, bk. 4, 32, 1848.
**Cherrykees.**—Weiser (1748) in Kauffman, West. Pa., app., 18, 1851.
**Chien, Nation du.**—Picquet (1752) in app. to Parkman, Montcalm and Wolfe, II, 417, 1884. (The Cherokees, according to Parkman.)
**Chirakues.**—Randolph (1699) in Rivers, South Carolina, 449, 1856.
**Chirokys.**—Writer *ca.* 1825 in Ann. de la Prop. de la Foi, II, 384, 1841.
**Chorakis.**—Document of 1748 in N. Y. Doc. Col. Hist., X, 143, 1858.
**Chreokees.**—Pike, Travels, 173, 1811. (*e* and *r* transposed.)
**Dog** (tribe).—Vaudreuil (1760) translated in N. Y. Doc. Col. Hist., X, 1094, 1858.
**Entari ronnon.**—Potier, Huron MS. Grammar, 1751. (One of their Wyandot names; equivalent to "Ridge people" or "Mountain people," Hewitt.)
**Gatohua.**—Gatschet (after Barton), Creek Mig. Leg., 28, 1884. (Delaware name.)
**Gattóchwa.**—Heckewelder in Barton, New Views, app. 8, 1798. (Delaware name, German form.)
**Isallanic** (race).—Schoolcraft in Ind. Aff. Rept., 73, 1849-50.
**Katowá.**—Gatschet, Creek Mig. Leg., I, 28, 1884. (Shawnee name; pl. Katowági.)
**Ketawaugas.**—Haywood, Nat. and Aborig. Tenn., 233, 1823. (Originally the name of a band, but extended to mean the whole tribe.)
**Kittuwa.**—Brinton, Lenape Legends, 16, 1885.
**Kitúhwakī'.**—Mooney, Cherokee MS. Voc. (B. A. E.), 1887. (Plural, Aní-Kitúhwakĭ'; originally the name of a Cherokee band, but used by Algonquian tribes to designate the whole tribe. See *Kituhwu*.)
**Kuttoowauw.**—Apaumut (1791) in Brinton, Lenape Legends, 16, 1885. (Mahican name.)
**Ochie'tari-ronnon.**—Potier, Huron MS. Grammar, 1751. (One of their Wyandot names.)
**Ojadagochroene.**—Livingston (1720) in N. Y. Doc. Col. Hist., V, 567, 1855.
**Ondadeonwas.**—Bleeker (1701) in ibid., IV, 918, 1854. (Same?)
**Oyadackuchraono.**—Weiser (1753) in ibid., VI, 795, 1855.
**Oyadagahroenes.**—Letter of 1713 in ibid., V, 386, 1855. (Incorrectly said to be the "Flatheads," a term here meaning the Catawba and allied tribes.)
**O-ya-dä'-go-o-no.**—Morgan, League of Iroquois, 337, 1851. (Iroquois name.)
**Oyatáge-ronóñ.**—Hewitt, oral information. (Iroquois name; practically alike in all six dialects: = "Inhabitants of the cave country." Oyáta = depression, hole, cave, in ground, in other dialects.)
**Oyaudah.**—Schoolcraft, Notes on Iroquois, 448, 1847. ("Cave people"; Seneca name.)
**Rechahecrians.**—Drake, Book of Inds., bk. 4, 22, 1848. (Name given by the Virginians in 1656 to an invading mountain tribe. Probably the Cherokee.)
**Rechehecrians.**—Rafinesque in Marshall, Kentucky, I, 36, 1824.
**Rickohockans.**—Lederer (1669) in Hawks, No. Carolina, II, 48, 1858. (Probably the Cherokee, as called by the Powhatan tribes. Rechahecrians is evidently the same word.)
**Shan-nack.**—Marcy, Red River, 273, 1854. (Wichita name.)
**Sulluggoes.**—Coxe, Carolana, 22, 1741.
**Talagans.**—Rafinesque in Marshall, Kentucky, I, 28, 1824. (= Talligewi.)
**Talegans.**—Ibid, 34.
**Talegawes.**—Ibid.
**Tallagewy.**—Schoolcraft, Ind. Tribes, II, 36, 1852.

**Choctaw.**—*Continued.*

Fourth division, or Choctaw branch, of the Muskhogean family. This branch included the Choctaw, Chickasaw, Houma, and some small tribes which formerly lived along Yazoo river. The languages of the members of this branch are so closely related that they may be considered as praetically identical (Gatschet, Creek Mig. Leg., 1, 53, 1884).

The earliest notice of these Indians is that recorded by De Soto. The giant Tuscalusa, whom he met in his march down Coosa valley, and carried to Mauvila, the capital of his province, was a Choctaw chieftain; and the Indians who fought the Spaniards so fiercely at this town were, in part at least, Choctaw. When the French, about the beginning of the 18th century, began to settle colonies at Mobile, Biloxi, and New Orleans, the Choctaw came early into friendly relations with them, and were their allies in their wars against other Indian tribes. In the French war on the Natches in 1730, a large body of Choctaw warriors served under a French officer. They continued this friendship until the English traders succeeded in drawing over to the English interest some of the eastern Choctaw towns. This brought on a war between them and the main body, who still adhered to the French, which continued until 1763, when peace was made between the two parties. The tribe was at war with the Creeks at various times, especially from 1765 to 1771, and it was also in constant warfare with the Chickasaw. After the French had surrendered their possessions to Great Britain in 1763, and to some extent previously thereto, members of the tribe began to move across the Mississippi to the west, where, in 1780, Milfort (Mémmoire, 95, 1802) met some of their bands who were then at war with the Caddq. About 1809 a Choctaw village existed on Wachita river, and another on Bayou Chicot, Opelousas parish, Louisiana. Morse (1820) says there were 1200 of them on the Sabine and Nechez rivers, and about 140 on Red river, near Nanatsoho (Rep. on Ind. Aff., 373, 1822). It is stated by some historians that this tribe, or parties of it, participated in the Creek war (Claiborne, Mississippi, 396); this, however, is emphatically denied by Halbert (Creek War of 1813 and 1814, 124), who states that he was informed (1877) by some of the oldest members of the tribe that the Choctaw showed no manifestation of hostility to the Americans during this war. The larger part of those in Mississippi began to migrate to Indian Territory in 1835, having ceded most of their lands to the United States in various treaties (see Royce, Indian Land Cessions, 18th Rep. Bur. Am. Eth., pt. 11).

The Choctaw were pre-eminently the agriculturists of the southern Indians. Though brave, their wars in most instances were defensive. No mention is made of the "great house," or "the square," in Choctaw towns, as they existed in the Creek communities, nor of the green-corn dance. The game of "chunke," as well as the game of ball, were played extensively among them. It was their custom to clean the bones of the dead before depositing in boxes or baskets in the bone-houses. This cleaning of the bones or removal of the flesh was performed by "certain old gentlemen with very long nails," who allowed their nails to grow long for this purpose. The people of this tribe also followed the custom of setting up poles around their new graves, on which they hung hoops, wreaths, etc., for the assistance of the spirit in its ascent. They followed the custom of flattening the head.

The population of the tribe when they first came into relation with the French, about the year 1700, has been estimated at from 15,000 to 20,000. The population in 1901 numbered 16,000, exclusive of 4250 "Choctaw Freedmen" (negroes). These are all under the Union agency, Indian Territory. The number of the remnant of the tribe still in Mississippi is not known.

There are, or at least were, formerly several dialects spoken in different sections; these, however, differed so little that they have not been considered worthy of special mention. The tribe was formerly divided into two sections: one, including the main body, formed the upper section, occupying the central portions of the state of Mississippi, and were always referred to and spoken of as the tribe. The others were known as the Gulf Coast Choctaw, who, according to Milfort (op. cit.), seem to have been somewhat inferior in culture to, and somewhat lower in morals than, their northern brethren.

According to Morgan (Ancient Society, 99, 162, 1877) the Choctaw were divided socially into two phratries, each including four gentes, as follows:

**Cherokee.**—*Continued.*

Tallegwi.—Rafinesque (1830?) in Mercer, Lenape Stone, 90, 1885.
Talligeú.—Heckewelder (1819) in ibid., 40.
Talligewi.—Walam Olum (1833) in Brinton, Lenape Leg., 200, 1885.
Talliké.—Brinton, Lenape Leg., 230, 1885. (Given as singular form of Talligewi. Zeisberger translates *talegán*, plural *talegáwak*, as "crane" in the Delaware language.)
Tchatakes.—La Salle (1682) in Margry, Découvertes, II, 197, 1877. (Evidently the Cherokee.)
Tsálagi.—Gatschet, Creek Mig. Leg., 25, 1884.
Tsâlâkĭ′.—Mooney, Cherokee MS. Voc. (B. A. E.), 1887. (Proper form, as used by the Upper Cherokee; plural, Aní-Tsálâkĭ′, abbreviated to Aní-Tsâlâk.)
Tsalakies.—Gallatin in Trans. Am. Antiq. Soc., II, 90, 1836.
Tsä-ló-kee.—Morgan, Anc. Soc., 113, 1877.
Tsárâgĭ′.—Mooney, Cherokee MS. Voc. (B. A. E.), 1887. (Proper form, as used by the Lower Cherokee; plural, Aní-Tsárâgĭ′.)
Tschirokesen.—Wrangell, Ethn. Nachrichten, xxiii, 1839.
Tsûlakkĭ.—Grayson, MS. Creek Vocab. (B. A. E.), 1885. (Creek name.)
Tzulukis.—Rafinesque, American Nations, I, 123, 1836.
Uwatáyo-róns.—Gatschet, Creek Mig. Leg., 28, 1884. ("Cave people"; Wyandot name.)
Uyáda.—Ibid. (Seneca name.)
Zolucans.—Rafinesque in Marshall, Kentucky, I, 23, 1824.
Zulocans.—Ibid.

**Chicago.**—A Miami village on the site of Chicago, Cook county, Illinois, at the period of the earliest explorations in that region, 1670–1700. A French document of 1695 makes it a Wea village at that time (N. Y. Doc. Col. Hist., IX, 619, 1855). It was also the name of a chief of the Illinois about 1725. The word is commonly translated as "wild onion place" or "skunk place," from *shikakua*, wild onion; or *shekaug*, skunk, in the neighboring Algonquian dialects. The name refers probably to the foul smell about the Chicago river. (See Hoffman in 14th Rep. Bur. Eth., p. 238.) (J.M.)

Checagou.—Tonty (1685) in Kelton, Ft. Mackinac, 119, 1884.
Chégagou.—Document of 1695 in N. Y. Doc. Col. Hist., IX, 619, 1855.
Chegakou.—La Hontan (1703), New Voy., I, 231, 1735.
Chekakou.—Ibid., I, 135, 1703.
Chicago.—Iberville (1702) in Minn. Hist. Soc. Coll., I, 341, 1872.
Chicags.—Croghan (1765) in N. Y. Doc. Col. Hist., VII, 785, 1856. (Misprint? It seems to have been then an Indian village.)
Chicagu.—St Cosme (1699) in Shea, Early Voy., 51, 1861.
Chicagou.—Document of 1695 in N. Y. Doc. Col. Hist., IX, 627, 1855.
Chicag8.—St Cosme (1699) in Shea, Early Voy., 56, 1861.
Chicagvv.—Ibid., 59.
Chicaqw.—Ibid., 52.
Chigagou.—Ibid., 68.
Chikago.—La Tour, map, 1784. (Indian village.)
Chikagons.—La Potherie, Hist. Amér., II, 346, 1753.
Chikagou.—St Cosme (1699) in Shea, Early Voy., 55, 1861.
Chikagoüa.—Gravier (1700) in ibid., 116–117.

**Chillicothe.**—One of the four territorial divisions of the Shawnee, and perhaps originally a phratry. The division is still recognized in the tribe, but the meaning of the word is lost. The division always occupied a village of the same name, and this village was regarded as the chief town of the tribe. As the Shawnee retreated westward before the whites, several villages of this name were successively occupied and abandoned. The old Lowertown, or "Lower Shawnee Town," at the mouth of the Scioto, in Ohio, was probably called Chillicothe. Besides this there were three other villages of that name in Ohio, viz.:

(1) On Paint creek, on the site of Oldtown, near Chillicothe in Ross county. This village may have been occupied by the Shawnee after removing from Lowertown. It was there as early as 1774, and was destroyed by the Kentuckians in 1787.

(2) On the Little Miami, about the site of Oldtown in Greene county. The Shawnee are said to have removed from Lowertown to this village, but it seems more probable that they went to the village on Paint creek. This village near Oldtown was frequently called Old Chillicothe, and Boone was a prisoner here in 1778. It was destroyed by Clark in 1780.

(3) On the (Great) Miami, at the present Piqua in Miami county. Destroyed by Clark in 1782. (J.M.)

Chellicotheé.—Perrin du Lac, Voy. des Deux Louisianas, 146, 1805.
Chilacoffee.—Broadhead (1779) in Penn. Archives, XII, 179, 1856.
Chilicothe.—Harmar (1790) in Kauffman, West. Pa., app., 226, 1851.
Chilikoffi.—Brodhead, op. cit., 181.
Chillacothe.—Harmar, op. cit., app., 227.
Chillicoffi.—Brodhead, op. cit., 258.
Chillicothe.—Clark (1782) in Butterfield, Wash. Irving Cor., 401, 1882.
Chilocathe.—Lang and Taylor, Rept., 22, 1843.
Paint Creek town.—Flint, Ind. Wars, 69, 1833. (In Ross county, on Paint creek.)
Shillicoffy.—Brodhead, op. cit., 258.
Tsalaxgásagi.—Gatschet, Shawnee MS. (B. A. E.), 1879. (Correct form in plural.)

**Choctaw.**—Probably a corrupted form of the Spanish word *chato*, meaning "flat" or "flattened," alluding to the custom of these Indians of flattening the head.

An important tribe of the Muskhogean stock, formerly occupying the middle and southern portions of what is now the state of Mississippi, their territory extending, in their most flourishing days, for some distance east of Tombigbee river. Mauvila, where De Soto met with such fierce resistance, was at that time in Choctaw territory. Ethnically they belong to Gatschet's

**Choctaw.**—*Continued.*
  A.—Kushap-okla, "divided people."
   1. Kush-iksa-, "reed gens."
   2. Law-okla.
   3. Lulak-iksa.
   4. Linoklusha.
  B.—Wataki hulata, "beloved people."
   1. Chufan-iksa-, "beloved people."
   2. Iskulani-, "small (people)."
   3. Chito-, "large (people)."
   4. Shakch-ukla, "cray-fish people."
  Besides these, mention is also made of a gens named "Urihesahe" (Wright, in Ind. Aff., Rep. for 1843, 348), which has not been identified; and of a local band—Oypat ukla—"eastern people" (q. v.).
  The Mobilian, Tohome (or Tomez), Touache, Mugulasha, Acolapissa (or Colapissa), Houma (or Ouma), and Conshac (q. v.), are classified by Gatschet (Creek Mig. Leg., I, 110–115, 1884) as offshoots from the Choctaw.
  Following are the names of the Choctaw villages: Allamutcha Old Town, Alloou Loanshaw, Ayanabi, Bayou chicot, Bishapa, Bishkoon, Bogue Chito, Bogue Toocola Chitto, Booctolooee, Boucfouca, Boutte Station, Cabea Hoola, Capinans, Chauki, Chicasawhay, Chinokabi, Chiskelikbatcha, Chomontokali, Chooca Hoola, Coatraw, Conachitow, Conchachitou, Congeeto, Cushtachas, Cutha Aimethaw, Cuthi Uckehaca, East Abeika, East Congeeto, East Yazoo Skatani, Ebita Poocolo Chitto, Ebita Poocolo Skatani, Etuck Chukke, Fuketcheepoonta, Fuluktabunnee, Haanka Ulla, Heitotowa, Hoola-tassa, Hyukkeni, Ikachiocata, Imongolasha Skatani, Kaffetalaya, Killis Tamaha, Little Colpissas, Lookfa, Lus'hapa, Mahewala, Nashoweya, Oka Altakkala, Oka Chippo, Oka Coopoly, Oka Hoola, Oka Lopassa, Oka Lusa, Oka Poolo, Okatallia, Oktibbeha, Olitassa, Oony, Oskelagna, Osuktalaya, Otakshanabe, Panthe, Pineshuk, Pooscoos te kale, Pooshapukanuk, Sapeessa, Schekahaw, Shanhaw, Skunnepaw, Sukinatchi, Talla, Talpahoka, Teakehaily Ekutapa, Tombigbee, Tonicahaw, West Abeika, West Imongolasha, West Yazoo, Wiatakali, Yagna Shoogawa, Yanatoe, Yowanne.
  The Choctaws apply the name *Ukla falaya* to a settlement of several towns, and *Ukla hannali* to a group of towns.  (A.S.G. C.T.)

**Cat Indians.**—Jefferys, French Dom., 135 (map), 1761.
**Chacatos.**—Barcia, Ensayo, 313, 1723.
**Chacktaws.**—Jefferson (1781), Notes, 144, 1825.
**Chactah.**—Rafinesque, Am. Nations, I, 241, 1836.
**Chactanys.**—Ann. Propagation de la Foi, II, 380, 1841.
**Chactas.**—Parraud, Hist. Kentucke, III, 1785.
**Chactaws.**—Jefferys, French Dom., I, 153, 1761.
**Chá'hta.**—Gatschet in American Antiquarian, IV, 76, 1881–82.
**Chaktaws.**—N. Y. Stat. at Large, Treaty of 1808, VII, 98, 1846.
**Chaltas.**—Coxe, Carolana, map, 1741. (Misprint.)
**Chaqueta.**—Iberville (1700) in Margry, Découvertes, IV, 463, 1880.
**Chaquitas.**—Ibid., 419.
**Chataw.**—Rogers, North America, 204, 1765.
**Chat-Kas.**—Du Pratz, Hist. La., II, 216, 1758.
**Chatkaws.**—Jefferys, French Dom., I, 165, 1761.
**Chattaes.**—Coxe, Carolana, map, 1741.
**Chattas.**—Ibid., 25.
**Chattoes.**—Ibid., 22.
**Chawetas.**—Perrin du Lac, Voy., 368, 1805.
**Chectaws.**—Morse, N. Am., 218, 1776.
**Chicktaws.**—Rogers, North America, 203, 1765.
**Chictaws.**—Ibid., 238.
**Chocataus.**—Disturnell, map Méjico, 1846.
**Chocktaws.**—Ellicott, Journal, 35, 1797.
**Chocta.**—Latham (1844) in Jour. Eth. Soc. London, I, 160, 1848.
**Choctaw.**—French writer (*ca.* 1727) in Shea, Cath. Missions, 429, 1855.
**Choctos.**—Domenech, Deserts, II, 193, 1860.
**Choktah.**—Barton, New Views, I, 1798.
**Choktaus.**—Am. Pioneers, I, 408, 1842.
**Choktaw.**—Boudinot, Star in West, 184, 1816.
**Chouactas.**—Martin, Hist. of La., I, 249, 1827.
**Chukaws.**—Boudinot, Star in West, 126, 1816.
**Flat Heads.**—Jefferys, French Dom., 135 (map), 1761.
**Flats.**—Bartram, Travels, 515, 1791.
**Nabuggindebaig.**—Tanner, Narrative, 316, 1830. ("Flat heads"; the name given by the Ottawas to a tribe "said to have lived below the Illinois river." Probably the same.)
**Shacktaus.**—Penhallow (1726) in N. H. Hist. Coll., 1st ser., 79, 1824.
**Shocktaus.**—Niles (1760) in Mass. Hist. Coll., 4th ser., 332, 1861.
**Tchacias.**—Charlevoix, Voy. to N. A., II, 210, 1766.
**Tchatakes.**—Margry, Découvertes, II, 197, 1877.
**Tchiactas.**—Bienville (1708) in Doc. Col. Hist. N. Y., IX, 925, 1855.
**Têtes Plates.**—Picquet's letter (1752) in Parkman, Montcalm and Wolfe, II, 417, 1884.
**Tschaktaer.**—Ally (1712), Historie der Reisen, XVI, 1758.
**Tshaxta.**—Müller, Grundriss der Sprachwissenschaft, II, pt. 1, 232, 1876.
**Tubbies.**—See under that name.

**Hominy.**—From the Algonquian dialects of New England; applied to a dish prepared from hulled flint corn pounded or cracked, and boiled with beans of various kinds, with meat or fish added. Some of the forms of the name given by early writers is *tackhummin*, "to grind corn (or grain)," and *pokhommin*, "to beat or thresh out."
(J.N.B.H.)

**Illinois.**—A confederacy of Algonquian tribes, the name of which, written successively by the early authorities Erinouaj, or Eriniwek (or -ouek), Liniwek (or -ouek), Aliniwek and Iliniwek, or Illinois, is derived from *ilini* or *illini*, "man" (*r* and *l* interchanged and -*ek*, -*ouek*, or -*wek* the plural termination, changed by the French to -*ois*). Hennepin

**Illinois.**—*Continued.*

states that the word *illini* signifies a "perfect or accomplished man." Although the term was used in the earliest notices as referring to a "nation," it applied in reality to a confederacy of several tribes formerly occupying the southern portion of Wisconsin, the northern part of Illinois, and certain sections of Iowa and Missouri. This account therefore relates only to the confederacy, the component tribes being treated under their respective names (Cahokia, Kaskaskia, Michigamea (Mouingouena), Peoria, and Tamaroa, q. v.).

The Illinois are first mentioned by the French writers (1640-58) as living in the vicinity of Green bay. But "vicinity" in this connection was a very indefinite term, and applied to tribes fifty or seventy-five leagues distant as well as to those in the immediate neighborhood. Whether Nicollet (1634-39) reached any of the tribes is not positively known. Justin Winsor (Cartier to Frontenac), judging by the language of Vimont (Jes. Rel., 1640), is inclined to think he did, and although it is doubtful whether he passed down Wisconsin river, this writer remarks that "it seems far more certain that Nicollet pushed directly south and reached the tribe of the Illinois, where he saw something of the Sioux, who were in that neighborhood on an expedition from the country farther west." The Jesuit Relation for 1660 represents them as living southwest from Green bay in sixty villages, and gives the extravagant estimate of the population as 20,000 men or 100,000 souls. Allouez, who met a body of them at La Pointe, on Lake Superior, says, "The Illinois do not live in these parts; their country is more than sixty leagues from here at the south beyond a great river." At the time of his visit some three or four years later, they were reduced to two villages in consequence of continual wars with the Sioux, Iroquois, and other tribes. It is evident, however, that he refers to those with whom he came in contact or of whom he obtained knowledge. There are no reliable data or native traditions relating to the direction from which they came, nor the point at which they entered the region in which they were first found by the whites. It is probable, however, that they came through the lower peninsula of Michigan, for they are not mentioned in the early accounts in connection with Mackinaw or Sault Ste Marie; it is known that the Mascoutin (q. v.), with whom they are probably related, came by this route; it is also generally conceded that the Sauk and Fox (q. v.), who, as well as the Mascoutin, were found in Wisconsin north of the Illinois, came by the same route; their somewhat close relationship with the Miami, who, with the Kickapoo and Mascoutin, are included by some of the old authorities under the term "Illinois," would seem to favor this view, as nothing is found indicating that either of these tribes was ever located at, or in, the vicinity of Mackinaw or the Sault. The statement in the Jesuit Relations that they came from the border of a great sea in the far west arose, no doubt (as Tailhan suggests), from a misunderstanding of the term "great water" given by the Indians, which in fact referred to the Mississippi. Their exact location when first heard of by the whites cannot be determined with certainty, as the tribes and bands were more or less scattered over southern Wisconsin, northern Illinois, and along the west bank of the Mississippi. They first came in actual contact with them (unless it be true that Nicollet visited them) at La Pointe (Chegoimegon), where Allouez met a party in 1667 which was visiting that point for purposes of trade. In 1670 the same priest found a number of them at the Mascoutin village on upper Fox river, some nine miles from where Portage City now stands, but this band then contemplated joining their brethren on the Mississippi. The different statements in regard to the number of their villages at this period and the indefiniteness as to localities render it difficult to reach a satisfactory conclusion on these points. It appears that some villages were located on the west side of the Mississippi, in what is now the state of Iowa, yet the larger portion of the tribes belonging to the confederacy resided at points in northern Illinois. When Marquette journeyed down the Mississippi in 1673, he found the Peoria and Moingouena on the west side, about the mouth of the Des Moines river. On his return he found them on Illinois river, near the site of the present city of Peoria. Thence he passed northward to the village of Kaskaskia, on upper Illinois river, within the limits of the present Lasalle county. At this time the

**Illinois.**—*Continued.*

village consisted of seventy-four cabins and was occupied by one tribe only, but a few years later (1690–94) missionaries reported it to consist of three hundred and fifty cabins, occupied by eight tribes. "Tribes," as used in this connection, probably signifies, in part at least, only bands. Father Sebastian Rale, who visited the village in 1692 and remained there two years, placed the number of cabins at three hundred, each of four "fires," with two families to a "fire," indicating a population of at least 10,000—probably an excessive estimate. The evidence, however, indicates that a large part of the confederacy was collected at this point for a while. The Kaskaskia at this time were in somewhat intimate relation with the Peoria, since Gravier, who returned to their village in 1700, says he found them preparing to start south, and believed if he could have arrived sooner "that the Kaskaskians would not thus have separated from the Peouaroua [Peoria] and other Illinois." By his persuasion they were induced to stop in southern Illinois at the point to which their name was given. It is evident that the Cahokia and Tamaroa were at this time located at their historic seats in southern Illinois. These Indians were almost constantly harassed by the Sioux, Foxes, and other northern tribes. It was probably on this account that they concentrated, about the time of La Salle's visit, on Illinois river. About the same time, or very soon thereafter, the Iroquois waged war against them which lasted several years and greatly reduced their numbers, while liquor obtained from the French tended still further to weaken them. The murder of the celebrated chief, Pontiac, by a Kaskaskia Indian about the year 1769, brought down the vengeance of the Lake tribes upon the Illinois, and a war of extermination was begun which in a few years reduced them to a mere handful, who took refuge with the French settlers at Kaskaskia, while the Sauk, Foxes, Kickapoo, and Potawatomi took possession of their country. In 1778 the Kaskaskia still numbered 210, living in a village three miles north of Kaskaskia, while the Peoria and Michigamea together numbered 170 on the Mississippi, a few miles farther up. According to Hutchins, both bands were demoralized and generally worthless. In 1833 the survivors, represented by the Kaskaskia and Peoria, sold their lands in Illinois and removed west of the Mississippi. They are now in Indian Territory, consolidated with the Wea and Piankashaw.

Nothing definite is known of their tribal divisions or clans. In 1736, according to Chauvignerie, the totem of the Kaskaskia was an arrow notched at the feather, or two arrows fixed like a St Andrew's cross, while the Illinois as a whole had the crane, bear, white hind, fork, and turtle totems.

The principal tribes or divisions of the Illinois were five in number: the Cahokia, Kaskaskia, Michigamea, Peoria, and Tamaroa. Among other divisions mentioned by the early writers are the Albivi, Amicoa, Amonokoa, Chepoussa, Chinko, Coiracoentanon, Espeminkia, Honabanou(?), Mosopelea (?), Mouingouena, Negaouichirinouek, Ocansa, Ochiakenend (?), Omouhoa, Pimitoui, and Tapouara. Some of these bands may have been parts of the Miami, Wea, or Piankashaw, who were closely connected with the Illinois. In general their villages bore the names of the tribes occupying them, and were constantly varying in number and shifting in location.

The Illinois are described by early writers as tall and robust, with rather pleasant visages. The descriptions of their character given by the early missionaries differ widely; Allouez and Marquette speak most highly of them, describing them as the most docile and susceptible of Christianity of any of the western Indians; while Membre and Marest describe them as wandering, idle, fearful, irritable, inconstant, traitorous, lewd, and brutal. Their history appears to justify the estimate of Marquette and Allouez, and it is well known that they were generally faithful to the French; on the other hand, they appear to have been timid and fearful, easily driven from their homes by their enemies, fickle, treacherous, and lewd. They were counted excellent archers, and, besides the bow, used in war a kind of pike and a wooden mace. Polygamy was common among them, a man sometimes taking several sisters as wives. Unfaithfulness of wives was punished, as among the Miami, the Sioux, and other tribes, by cutting off the nose; and as the men were very jealous, this punishment was often inflicted on mere suspicion (Membre, Nar.). The husband was

**Illinois.**—*Continued.*
not prone to separate from his wife after children were born to them; in case of separation the children remained with the mother. It was not the custom of the Illinois at the time the whites first became acquainted with them to bury their dead. The body was wrapped in skins and attached by the feet and head to trees. There is reason, however, to believe, from discoveries which have been made in mounds and ancient graves, which appear to be attributable to some of the Illinois tribes, that the skeletons, after the flesh had rotted away, were buried, often in rude stone sepulchers; and that after they had been in contact with the whites for some time, probably through the influence of the missionaries, inhumation became the usual custom. The prisoners they captured in war were usually sold to other tribes. Little is known in regard to their religious beliefs. The Peoria declared to Gravier that all of man died; that if the spirit survived they would see the dead return to earth.

According to Hennepin the cabins of the more northern tribes were made like long arbors and covered with double mats of flat flags, or rushes, so well sewed that they were never penetrated by wind, snow, or rain. To each cabin were four or five fires, and to each fire two families, indicating that each dwelling housed some eight or ten families. Their towns were not inclosed.

All accounts agree that the Illinois when first known were numerous and powerful, but the early estimates of their population are too vague to be reliable. It is probable that the earlier writers classed with the Illinois many bands afterward recognized as distinct tribes. This would account in some measure for the exaggerated accounts of their early numbers. Hennepin estimated them about 1680 at 400 houses and 1800 warriors, or about 7000 souls. The constant wars waged against them by other tribes, and the vices introduced by the French, rapidly reduced them, but about the year 1750 they were still estimated at from 1500 to 2000 souls. They were practically exterminated by the war following the death of Pontiac, and in 1800 there were only about 150 left. In 1885 the consolidated Peoria, Kaskaskia, Wea, and Piankashaw numbered but 149, and even these are much mixed with white blood. The subsequent history of the tribes is noticed under their respective names, as above given.

The villages of the confederacy noted in history are: Cahokia (mission), Immaculate Conception, Kaskaskia, Matchinkoa, Moingwena, Mosopelea, Peoria, Pimitoui. (J.M. C.T.)

**Abimiouec.**—Document of 1660, in Margry, Découvertes, I, 54, 1875. (*b* should be *l*.)
**Abimi8ec.**—Jesuit Relations, 12, 1660. (*b* should be *l*. It is corrected in the errata, but the incorrect form is followed in Margry.)
**Alimouek.**—Ibid., 21, 1667.
**Alimouk.**—Ibid., III, index, 1858.
**Aliniouek.**—Ibid., 21, 1658.
**Alini8ek.**—Ibid., 12, 1660. (Correction in errata.)
**Alinoueckes.**—Coxe, Carolana, 19, 1741.
**Allinouecks.**—Ibid., 49.
**Chichigoueks.**—La Potherie, Hist. Am., II, 49, 1753.
**Chicktaghicks.**—Colden (1727), Five Nations, 30, 1747.
**Chictaghicks.**—Smith in Williams, Vermont, I, 501, 1809. (Iroquois name.)
**Chigtaghcicks.**—Colden (1727), Five Nations, 31, 1747.
**Chiktachiks.**—Homann, map, 1756.
**Eriniouai.**—Jesuit Relations, 35, 1640.
**Eriniwek.**—Ibid., III, index, 1858.
**Geghdageghroano.**—Post (1758) in Proud, Pa., II, app., 113, 1798.
**Geghtigeghroones.**—Canajoharie conf. (1759) in N. Y. Doc. Col. Hist., VII, 384, 1856.
**Hilini.**—Brinton, Lenape Leg., 213, 1885.
**Hiliniki.**—Rafinesque, Am. Nations, I, 139, 1836. (Delaware name.)
**Ilimouek.**—Jesuit Relations, 101, 1670.
**Iliné.**—Hervas (1785) in Vater, Mith., pt. 3, sec. 3, 347, 1816. (Italian form.)
**Ilinese.**—La Hontan, New Voy., I, 217, 1703.
**Ilinesen.**—Walch, map, 1805. (German form.)
**Iliniouek.**—Jesuit Relations, 19, 1667.
**Ilinois.**—Ibid., 86, 1670.
**Ilinouets.**—Ibid., 93, 1670.
**Ilinouetz.**—Ibid., 101, 1670.
**Ilionois.**—Proud, Pa., II, 296, 1798.
**Illenois.**—Morse, North Am., map, 1776.
**Illenonecks.**—Ibid., 255.
**Illicoüeck.**—Coxe, Carolana, 17, 1741.
**Illimoüec.**—Jesuit Relations, 21, 1667.
**Illinese.**—Hennepin, Cont. of New Disc., 88, 1698.
**Illinesen.**—Vater, Mith., pt. 3, sec. 3, 341, 1816. (German form.)
**Il-li-ni.**—Hough in Indiana Geol. Rept., map, 1883.
**Illiniens.**—Hennepin, Cont. of New Disc., 45b, 1698.
**Illiniwek.**—Shea, Cath. Miss., 348, 1855.
**Illinoias.**—Niles (1761?) in Mass. Hist. Soc. Coll., 4th ser., V, 541, 1861.
**Illinois.**—Prise de Possession (1671) in Margry, Découvertes, I, 96, 1875.
**Illinoix.**—Brackenridge, La., 132, 1815.
**Illinonecks.**—Morse, North Am., 255, 1776.
**Illinoneeks.**—Document of 1719 in N. C. Rec., II, 351, 1886.
**Illinouecks.**—Coxe, Carolana, 49, 1741.
**Illonese.**—Schermerhorn (1812) in Mass. Hist. Soc. Coll., 2d ser., II, 3, 1814.
**Illonois.**—Campbell (1761) in ibid., 4th ser., IX, 423, 1871.
**Illuni.**—Allouez (1665) *fide* Ramsey in Ind. Aff. Rept., 71, 1849-50.
**Irinions.**—Jesuit Relations, 97, 1642.
**Isle aux Noix.**—Lapham, Ind's of Wis., 4, 1870. ("Walnut island"; a form used by some author, who probably mistook Illinois for a corrupted French word.)
**Islinois.**—La Salle (1680) in Margry, Découvertes, II, 33, 1877.
**Kichtages.**—Maryland treaty (1682) in N. Y. Doc. Col. Hist., III, 325, 1853.

# DICTIONARY OF INDIANS.

**Illinois.**—*Continued.*
**Kicktages.**—Albany conference (1726) in ibid., v, 791, 1855.
**Kighetawkigh Roanu.**—Dobbs, Hudson Bay, 28, 1744. (Iroquois name.)
**Kightages.**—Livingston (1720) in N. Y. Doc. Col. Hist., v, 567, 1855.
**Lazars.**—Croghan (1759) in Kauffman, West. Pa., 146, 1851.
**Lezar.**—Ibid. in Jefferson, Notes, 145, 1825. (Seems to be the Illinois.)
**Liniouek.**—Jesuit Relations, 30, 1656.
**Linneways.**—Brice, Ft. Wayne, 121, 1868.
**Linways.**—Croghan, op. cit.
**Minneways.**—Brice, Ft. Wayne, 121, 1868.
**Ondataouaouat.**—Potier in CharleVoix, New France, II, 270, 1866. (First applied by the Wyandot to the Ottawa (q. V. for forms), but afterward to the Illinois.)
**Willinis.**—Proud, Pa., II, 296, 1798.
**Witishaxtánu.**—Gatschet, Wyandot MS. (B. A. E.), 1881. (From Ushaxtáno, Illinois river; Wyandot name for the Peoria, Kaskaskia, Wea, and Piankashaw.)

**Milwaukee.**—"The fine land" (from *milo* or *mino*, "good," and *aki*, "land" —Baraga). Kelton (Annals Ft. Mackinac, 1884) gives the form as *Minewagi*, meaning "there is a good point," or "there is a point where huckleberries grow." About the year 1699 a village, known under some form of this name, and perhaps belonging to the Potawatomi, existed near the present Milwaukee, Wisconsin.
(J.M.)

**Melleki.**—Old map (1699?), followed in map in Lapham, Ind's of Wis., 1870.
**Melwarck.**—St Cosme (1699) in ibid., 5.
**Melwarik.**—Lapham, ibid., 20. (Probably from St Cosme, 1699.)

**Nashua.** A tribe formerly living on upper Nashua river, in Worcester county, Massachusetts, and said by some writers to have been connected with the Massachuset tribe, but classed by Potter with the Pennacook. They had a village, also called Nashua, near the present Leominster, but their principal village seems to have been Weshacum, a few miles farther south. They were the original owners of the Naushawag or Nashua tract, extending for several miles in every direction around Lancaster. On the outbreak of King Philip's war in 1675 they joined the hostile Indians, and at his death the Nashua, numbering several hundred, attempted to escape in two bodies to the east and west. Both parties were pursued and a large number killed and captured, the prisoners being afterward sold into slavery. A few of those who escaped eastward joined the Pennacook, while about 200 of the others crossed the Hudson and fled to the Mahican or the Munsee, and ceased to exist as a separate tribe. A few still remained near their old homes in 1701. (J.M.)

**Nashaway.**—Eliot (1651) in Mass. Hist. Soc. Coll., 3d ser., IV, 123, 1834.
**Nashawog.**—Eliot (1648) in ibid., 81, 1834.
**Nashoway.**—Report (ca. 1657) in N. H. Hist. Soc. Coll., III, 96, 1832.
**Nashua.**—Writer of 1810 in Mass. Hist. Soc. Coll., 2d ser., I, 181, 1814.
**Nashuays.**—Drake, Book of Ind's, IX, 1848.
**Nashuway.**—Hinckley (1676) in Mass. Hist. Soc. Coll., 4th ser., V, I, 1861.
**Nashuyas.**—Domenech, Deserts, I, 442, 1860.
**Nassawach.**—Courtland (1688) in N. Y. Doc. Col. Hist., III, 562, 1853.
**Nasshaway.**—Pynchon (1677) in ibid., XIII, 511, 1881.
**Nassoway.**—Writer of 1676 in Drake, Ind. Chron., 130, 1836.
**Naushawag.**—Paine (about 1792) in Mass. Hist. Soc. Coll., 1st ser., I, 115, 1806. (Applied to the territory.)
**Weshakim.**—Gookin (1674) in Mass. Hist. Soc. Coll., 1st ser., I, 193, 1806.

**Niagara.**—Being of Iroquoian origin, one of the earliest forms of this place-name is that in the Jesuit Relation for 1641, in which it is written *Onguiaahra*, evidently a misprint for *Ongniaahra*, and it is there made the name of a Neutral town and of the river which to-day bears this designation, although *Ongmarahronon* of the Jesuit Relation for the year 1640 appears to be a misprint for *Ongniarahronon*, signifying "People of *Ongniarah*." The Iroquois and their congeners applied it to the place whereon the village of Youngstown, Niagara county, New York, now stands. On the Tabula Novæ Franciæ, or Map of New France, in Historiæ Canadensis, sev Novæ-Franciæ (bk. 10, Paris, 1664, but made in 1660 by Franciscus Creuxius, S. J.), the Falls of Niagara are called "*Ongiara catarractes*." Much ingenuity has been exercised in attempts to analyze this name. The most probable derivation, however, is from the Iroquoian sentence-word, which in Onondaga and Seneca becomes *O'hniä'gä'*, and in Tuscarora *U'hnia'kā'r*, and which signifies "bisected bottom-land." Its first use was perhaps by the Neutral or Huron tribes. (J.N.B.H.)

**Ohio.**—The Abbé de Gallinée in 1669 employed this Iroquoian river name in its present orthography (Margry, Découvertes, pt. I, 114). Ten years later La Salle, in speaking of the stream, says (op. cit., pt. II, 79–80), "a river which I have found," and then, a little farther, he adds, "which I have called *Baudrane*. The Iroquois call it Ohio, and the Outaouas [Ottawas] Olighin-cipou." But in the Acte de Prise de Possession (op. cit., pt. II, 184), dated March 13, 1682, he writes,

**Ohio.**—*Continued.*
"from the mouth of the river Saint-Louis, called Ohio, Olighin-sipou and Chukagoua." The latter name is also written *Suskakoua* (op. cit., pt. II, 96). It was most probably a name of Cumberland river.

The name Ohio is evidently a compressed form of the common Iroquoian sentence-word O'hio<sup>n</sup>'hiio', signifying "It-river is fine, beautiful." It is derived from the noun o'hio<sup>n</sup>'hä̆', "it-river, it-stream"; the prefixed *o* is a gender sign, and the adjective *-iio'*, "fine, beautiful," the substantive verb being understood. Hence, Ohio signifies, "It is a beautiful river."
(J.N.B.H.)

**Pontiac.**—An Ottawa chief, born about 1720, probably on Ottawa river, Canada. Though his paternity is not positively established, it is most likely that his father was an Ottawa chief and his mother an Ojibwa woman. J. Wimer (Events in Ind. Hist., 155, 1842), says that as early as 1746 he commanded the Indians—mostly Ottawa—who defended Detroit against the attack of the northern tribes. It is supposed he led the Ottawa and Ojibwa warriors at Braddock's defeat. He first appears prominently in history at his meeting with Maj. Robert Rogers, in 1760, at the place where Cleveland, Ohio, now stands. This officer had been despatched to take possession of Detroit on behalf of the English. Pontiac objected to the further invasion of the territory, but, learning that the French had been defeated in Canada, consented to the surrender of Detroit to the English, and was the means of preventing an attack on the latter by a body of Indians at the mouth of the strait. That which gives him most prominence in history and forms the chief episode of his life is the plan he devised for a general uprising of the Indians and the destruction of the forts and settlements of the English. He was for a time disposed to be on terms of friendship with the English and consented to acknowledge King George, but only as an "uncle," not as a superior. Failing to receive the recognition he considered his due as a great sovereign, and being deceived by the rumor that the French were preparing for the reconquest of their American possessions, he resolved to put his scheme into operation. Having brought to his aid most of the tribes northwest of the Ohio, his plan was to make a sudden and contemporaneous attack on all the British posts on the lakes,—at St. Joseph, Ouiatenon, Michilimackinac, and Detroit,—the Miami and Sandusky, and also on the forts at Niagara, Presque Isle, Le Bœuf, Venango, and Pitt (Du Quesne). The taking of Detroit was to be his special task. The end of May, 1763, was the appointed time when each tribe was to attack the nearest fort, and, after killing the garrison, to fall on the adjacent settlements. It was not long before the posts at Sandusky, St. Joseph, Miami (Ft.Wayne), Ouiatenon, Michilimackinac, Presque Isle, Le Bœuf, and Venango were taken and the garrison in most cases massacred; but the main points, Detroit and Fort Pitt, were successfully defended and the Indians forced to raise the siege. This was a severe blow to Pontiac, but his hopes were finally crushed by the receipt of a letter from M. Neyon, commander of Ft. Chartres, advising him to desist from further warfare, as peace had been concluded between France and Great Britain. However, unwilling to abandon entirely his hope of driving back the English, he made an attempt to incite the tribes along the Mississippi to join in another effort. Being unsuccessful in this attempt, he finally made peace at Detroit, August 17, 1765. In 1769 he attended a drinking carousal at Cahokia, Illinois, where he was murdered by a Kaskaskia Indian. Pontiac, if not fully the equal of Tecumseh, stands closely second to him in strength of mind and breadth of comprehension. (C.T.)

**Raccoon.**—From the southern Algonquian group of dialects. By the early Virginia authors it is variously written *rahaughcums*, *raugroughcuns*, *arocouns, aroughcuns, rarowcuns, rakowns, racones, arrahacounes*. This well-known animal is described as being "much like a badger, but living on trees like a squirrel." (J.N.B.H.)

**Samp.**—The name of a dish prepared from pounded or cracked corn with the flour or finest portion sifted out of it, and boiled with beans or pieces of meat or fish, or with all of these. From the Algonquian dialects of New England, *sampe* and *nawsauinp* being among the early forms used.
(J.N.B.H.)

**Squash.**—The present name of this well-known vegetable is from the Algonquian dialects spoken in New Eng-

**Squash.**—*Continued.*
land. Early authors wrote the name in a variety of ways, among them being *squantersquash* and *squantersquashes*, *askutasquashes*, *isquontersquoashes*, *isquotersquashes*, and *isquoukersquashes*. In English usage the fore-part of the Indian term has been discarded. (J.N.B.H.)

**Succotash.**—From the Algonquian dialects of New England, written *msickquatash* by Roger Williams. The dish consisted of the whole grains of green corn cut or scraped from the cob, with which beans of various kinds were usually mixed, and boiled as a stew or pudding. (J.N.B.H.)

**Susquehanna.**— Algonquian in origin, this river name was written *Sasquesahanocks* by Capt. John Smith in 1606; but in this form it is hybrid, the final *s* being the English suffix indicating the plural form of nouns. *Sasquesahanock* is then the aboriginal form with which present inquiry is concerned, but this appellation is sometimes written *Sasquehanna;* both, however, are correct. *Sasquesa* is a derivative adjective form of *asisku* or *asiskwa*, signifying "mud or clay," and means therefore "muddy or roily." But the bare noun may also be employed in compounds with an adjective force, giving rise to the second form of the term in question. The next element is *han* or *hanna*, meaning "river or stream of water"; and the last is *ock*, a locative suffix, signifying, "at," "at the place of." Hence, *Susquehanna* signifies, "At the roily or muddy river." Smith thus applied a place-name to a people. (J.N.B.H.)

**Tecumseh,** more strictly Tecumthé.— A celebrated Shawnee chief, born in 1768 at a former Indian village on Mad river, near Springfield, Ohio. His father, Puckeshinwa, was a member of the Kiscopoke (Tiger?) gens of the tribe and his mother, Methoataske, of the Turtle gens. His father rose to the rank of chief, and fell in the battle of the Kanawha in 1774. After the death of his father Tecumseh was placed in charge of his oldest brother, Cheeseekau, who, it is said, labored to lead him to a high Indian standard of a warrior's life. He seems to have had a passion for war from his boyhood. Previous to 1791 he took part in some war expeditions to the south and west, and during 1792–93 joined in several forays on the white settlements and in resisting the attack of the Kentucky volunteers. He took an active part in the Indian effort to resist Anthony Wayne. About 1805 or 1806 he began, in connection with his brother Elskwatawa, the "Prophet," to develop his scheme of uniting the western tribes in an effort to resist the further advance of the whites. He claimed that the whole country belonged to the tribes in common, hence a sale of land to the whites by one tribe did not convey title unless confirmed by the other tribes. He therefore seriously protested against the cession of lands made about that time to the whites by the Miami and other tribes, or, as is probable, these were used as a pretext for advancing his scheme of united effort. Another part of his program, probably in part the offering of his brother's mind, was that there should be no more fighting between tribes, the people should abandon the use of intoxicating liquors, and wear skins instead of blankets as their ancestors had done. The various tribes from the Great Lakes to the Gulf were visited and the plan unfolded to them. General W. H. Harrison, then governor of Northwest Territory, warned the movers in this scheme to desist, and held several interviews with Tecumseh, but these efforts were productive of no steps toward peace. The war began, but Tecumseh's plans were blasted by the defeat of the Indians at Tippecanoe, which was brought on by his brother while Tecumseh was absent in the south and contrary to his positive order. After this he joined the English and was killed at the battle of the Thames, Oct. 5, 1813. In estimating the character of Tecumseh the language of Trumbull (Indian Wars) may be accepted with assurance: "He was the most extraordinary Indian that has appeared in history [of the United States]. He would have been a great man in any age or nation. Independent, of the most consummate courage and skill as a warrior, and with all the characteristic acuteness of his race, he was endowed by nature with the attributes of mind necessary for great political combinations." Although enthusiastic in behalf of what he believed to be for the welfare of his race, he was not blind to the power of the United States. He was aware that the only hope of preventing a further advance of the whites was by a union of the tribes. He discarded the idea of the right of discovery and

**Tecumseh.**—*Continued.*
superior civilization by which European powers claimed dominion, and artfully advanced the theory of the communal right of the tribes to the entire country. He admitted that the title of a given tribe within the limits was perfect and perpetual as to other tribes, but held that this did not confer upon the tribe the right to sell to others not Indians, this right belonging alone to the whole body. As this was followed up by a plea to the tribes to cease war between themselves, and break off from indulgence in intoxicating drinks, we have evidence of a mind with great comprehensive powers. See Mooney in Fourteenth Rep. Bur. Eth., 681-691. (C.T.)

**Treaties.** — The political status of the Indians residing within the territorial limits of the United States has been changed in one important respect by official action. From the formation of the Government to March 3, 1871, the relations with the Indians were determined by treaties made with their tribal authorities; but by act of Congress of the date named the legal fiction of recognizing the tribes as independent nations with which the United States could enter into solemn treaties was finally set aside after it had continued for nearly a century. The effect of this act was to bring under the immediate control of Congress the relations of the Government with the Indians and to reduce to simple agreements what had before been accomplished by treaties as with a foreign power. Why the Government, although claiming complete sovereignty over the territory and inhabitants within its domain, adopted the method of dealing with the Indians through treaties, which in the true legal sense of the term can only be entered into by independent sovereignties, may briefly be stated:

The first step of the Government in determining its policy toward the Indians, whether expressed or implied, was to decide as to the nature of their territorial rights, this being the chief factor in their relations with the whites. This decision is distinctly stated by the United States Supreme Court in the case of Johnson and Graham's lessee *vs.* McIntosh (8 Wheaton, 453 et seq.), as follows: "It has never been contended that the Indian title amounted to nothing. Their right of possession has never been questioned. The claim of the Government extends to the complete, ultimate title, charged with the right of possession, and to the exclusive power of acquiring this right." The next step was to determine the branch of the Government to carry out this policy. By the 9th of the Articles of Confederation it was declared that "the United States in Congress assembled have the sole and exclusive right and power of regulating the trade, and managing all affairs with the Indians not members of any of the states." It is clear, therefore, that while acting under the Articles of Confederation the right of managing relations with the Indians resided in Congress alone. In the formation of the Constitution this is briefly expressed under the powers of the legislative department, as follows: "To regulate commerce with foreign nations and among the several states, and with the Indian tribes."

It is apparent, from the use of the term "tribes," that the framers of the Constitution had in contemplation the method of dealing with the Indians as tribes through treaties. This is clearly shown by the act of March 1, 1793, in which it is stated that no purchase or grant of lands shall be of any validity "unless the same be made by a treaty or convention entered into pursuant to the Constitution." This action of Congress necessarily placed the initiatory steps in dealing with the Indians under the jurisdiction of the President as the treaty-making power, subject to confirmation by the Senate.

The colonies and also the mother country had treated with the Indians as "nations," their chiefs or sachems often being designated as "kings,"— and this idea, being retained by the founders of our Government, was ingrafted into their policy. It must be remembered that the colonies then were weak, and that the Indian tribes were comparatively strong and capable of requiring recognition of equality. Notwithstanding the evident anomaly of such course, the growth in numbers and strength of the whites, and the diminishing power of the natives, this implied equality was recognized in the dealings between the two until the act of March 3, 1871. During all this time Indian titles to lands were extinguished only under the treaty-making clause of the Constitution; and these treaties, though the tribe may have been reduced to a small band, were usually clothed in the same stately verbiage as the most

**Treaties.**—*Continued.*
important treaty with a great European power.

It appears from the annual report of the Commissioner of Indian Affairs for 1890 that "From the execution of the first treaty made between the United States and the Indian tribes residing within its limits (September 17, 1778, with the Delawares) to the adoption of the act of March 3, 1871, that 'no Indian nation or tribe within the territory of the United States shall be acknowledged or recognized as an independent nation, tribe, or power with whom the United States may contract by treaty,' the United States has pursued a uniform course of extinguishing the Indian title only with the consent of those tribes which were recognized as having claim to the soil by reason of occupancy, such consent being expressed in treaties. . . . Except only in the case of the Sioux Indians in Minnesota, after the outbreak of 1862, the Government has never extinguished an Indian title as by right of conquest; and in this case the Indians were provided with another reservation, and subsequently were paid the net proceeds arising from the sale of the land vacated."

From the same report it is learned that the Indian title to all the public domain had then been extinguished except in Alaska, in the portions included in one hundred and sixty-two reservations, and those acquired by the Indians through purchase. As the title to reservations is derived in most cases from the United States, and title by purchase is derived directly or indirectly from the same source, it may be stated that the Indian title to all the public domain, except in Alaska, had practically been extinguished by the year 1890.

As the dealings with Indians regarding lands constitute the most important transactions with which the Government has been concerned, and those to which most of the treaties relate, the Indian policy of the United States is most clearly shown thereby. By some of the European Governments having American colonies,—as, for example, Spain,—the Indian claim was recognized only to as much land as was occupied or in use, but it has been usual for the United States to allow it to extend to the territory claimed, where the boundaries were recognized and acknowledged by the surrounding tribes. It would seem, in fact, that the United States proceeded on the theory that *all* the land within their territorial bounds were held by the natives, and hence that the possessory right of the Indians thereto must be extinguished. The only known variation from this rule was in the case of the Uintah Utes, where an omitted portion of their claimed territory was taken possession of (Eighteenth Rep. Bur. Am. Eth., pt. II, 824, 1896–97). From the formation of the Government up to March 3, 1871, six hundred and fifty-three treaties were made with ninety-eight different tribes or recognized tribal organizations, as follows:

Apache.
Appalachicola.
Arapaho.
Arikara.
Bannock.
Blackfoot.
Brothertown.
Blood.
Caddo.
Cahokia.
Cayuse.
Chasta.
Cherokee.
Cheyenne.
Chickasaw.
Chippewa.
Choctaw.
Comanche.
Cow Creek.
Creek.
Crow.
Delaware.
Dwamish.
Eel River.
Flathead.
Fox.
Grosventres.
Iowa.
Kalapuya.
Kansa.
Kaskaskia.
Kickapoo.
Kiowa.
Klamath.
Kutenai.
Makah.
Mandan.
Mdewakanton.
Menominee.
Miami.
Miniconjou.
Missouri.
Michigamea.
Modoc.
Mohawk.
Molala.
Munsee.
Navaho.
Nez Percé.
Nisqualli.
Oglala.
Omaha.
Oneida.
Hunkpapa.
Osage.
Oto.
Ottawa.
Pawnee.
Peoria.
Piankashaw.
Piegah.
Ponca.
Potawatomi.
Puyallup.
Quapaw.
Quinaielt.
Rogue River.
Sauk.
Seminole.
Seneca.
Shawnee.
Shomamish.
Shoshoni.
Sioux.
Sklallam.
Stockbridge.
Suquamish.
Tamaroa.
Tawakoni.
Teton.
Tuscarora.
Two Kettles.
Umatilla.
Umpqua.
Pend d'Oreille.
Ute.
Wahpekute.
Wahpeton.
Wallawalla.
Wasco.
Wea.
Winnebago.
Wichita.
Wyandot.
Yakima.
Yankton.
Yanktonai.

**Treaties.**—*Continued.*

A natural sequence to treaties relating in whole or in part to lands (being fully twenty-four twenty-fifths of the whole number) was the establishment of reservations, either within the original territory or elsewhere. Up to 1890, by which time the Indian title had practically been extinguished to all lands in the United States except Alaska and the portions of the reservations retained by the grantors in the original cessions, one hundred and sixty-two of these reservations had been established. Of these, according to the Report of the Commissioner of Indian Affairs for 1890, there were established:

56 By executive order.
6 By executive order under authority of Congress.
28 By act of Congress.
15 By treaty, with boundaries defined or enlarged by executive order.
5 By treaty or agreement and act of Congress.
1 By unratified treaty.
51 By treaty or agreement.

It appears from this list that the method of establishing reservations has not been uniform, some being by treaty, some by executive order, and others by act of Congress. Those established by executive order, independent of the act of Congress, were not held to be permanent before the "general allotment act of 1887, under which the tenure has been materially changed, and all reservations, whether by executive order, act of Congress, or treaty, are held permanent." Reservations by executive order under authority of an act of Congress are those which have been authorized or established by acts of Congress and their limits defined by executive order, or have been first established by executive order and subsequently confirmed by Congress.

Other respects in which the power of Congress intervenes in reference to Indian lands, or is necessary to enable the Indians to carry out their desires in regard thereto, are the following:

(1) Allotments of land in severalty previous to the act of February 8, 1887, could be made only by treaty or by virtue of an act of Congress, but by this act general authority is given to the President for this purpose.

(2) Leases of land, sale of standing timber, granting of mining privileges, and right of way to railroads are all prohibited to the Indians without some enabling act of Congress. On the other hand, it is obligatory on the Government to prevent any intrusion, trespass, or settlement on the lands of any tribe of Indians except where their consent has been given by agreement or treaty.

For the treaties relating to cessions of lands between the United States and the Indians, see the Eighteenth Annual Report of the Bureau of American Ethnology, pt. II, 1899.
(C.T.)

**Wyandot.**—The correct form seems to be Wandót. According to Morgan it means "calf of the leg," and refers to a peculiar manner of cutting meat. Information obtained from a Wyandot source by Gatschet appears to confirm this rendering. The modern Wyandots include the remains of the Wyandots proper, known as Hurons to the early French writers, and of the Tionontatis (q. v.), who probably outnumbered the Wyandots when the two tribes united in 1650 and abandoned their country to escape the Iroquois. As late as 1721 the Tionontatis still had their separate name and chieftaincy, but all tribal distinctions have long since been lost. Huron, their French name, comes from *hure*, "a wild boar's crest," the peculiar manner in which the Hurons arranged their hair having suggested to the early French the bristles of a wild boar. They were also called sometimes Bons Iroquois, or "good Iroquois," to distinguish them from the cognate tribes in New York, who were hostile to the French. The Delawares called them Delamatteno, but the Algonquian tribes generally called them Nadowa (q. v.), or "snakes," a name applied to all tribes not of Algonquian stock, and especially to the Iroquoian tribes. Their present name first came into general use after the removal of a part of the tribe from Detroit to Sandusky, Ohio, in 1751.

When first known to the French, about 1615, the Hurons occupied a narrow territory between Georgian bay and Lake Simcoe, in Simcoe county, Ontario. They had about twenty villages, but the number and location of these settlements were constantly changing, as it was the custom of the tribe to abandon their old villages and build new ones at regular intervals of time. Their numbers were estimated all the way from 10,000 to 30,000 souls, and it seems probable that they were at least as

**Wyandot.**—*Continued.*

numerous as the confederated Iroquois, by whom their organization was afterward destroyed. A few years previous to their first war with the Iroquois they had been greatly weakened by smallpox and other epidemics. The Hurons proper consisted of three·"nations"—probably phratries or gentes—viz.: Attigouantan, Arendarhonon, and Attignenonghac, known respectively to the French as the nations of the Bear, Rock, and Cord, the Bear nation being the first in numbers and importance. Another tribe, the Tohotaenrat, was confederated with the Hurons, besides which two other small tribes, the Wenrorono and Totontaratonhronon, had taken refuge with them before 1640 to escape the ravages of the Iroquois. Immediately adjoining the Hurons on the southwest were their allies, the Tionontatis, with whom they afterward united. All three tribes were of Iroquoian stock, excepting the Tohontaratonhronon, who were Algonquian.

When the French established themselves at Montreal the Hurons and other tribes were in the habit of making periodical trips down the Ottawa river to its mouth, for the purpose of trading with the Montagnais of the lower St. Lawrence, who came up to meet them. On one of these occasions they invited the missionaries into their country, and in 1623 the invitation was accepted by the Recollets. Two years later the Jesuits entered the field and through their efforts the Huron mission soon became the most important within the French dominions in America. Their success, however, excited the jealousy of the Iroquois, who had long been awaiting an opportunity to avenge upon the French the defeat which they had suffered at the hands of Champlain in 1609. They were also the enemies of the Hurons, and, according to Sagard, large war parties of the latter tribe frequently invaded and ravaged the country of the Iroquois. The mutual hatred was doubtless intensified by the fact that the Hurons had sheltered from the wrath of the Iroquois the small tribes already mentioned. Historians generally have represented the destruction of the Hurons as the result of an unexpected and unprovoked war waged against them by the Iroquois, but in reality it was but the final act in a struggle which was already in progress when the French first settled in Canada. The fire-arms which the Iroquois could now procure from the Dutch enabled them to give the finishing blow to the Hurons, and their success in this war probably led them to enter upon that career of conquest which soon brought under their dominion ·half the country east of the Mississippi.

In July, 1648, the Iroquois began the final war by attacking and destroying the important village of Teananstayae and killing the resident missionary. This was followed up by other attacks until the Hurons were compelled to scatter in small parties, many of them joining the Tionontatis. The enemy ranged the country all winter, and early in 1649 destroyed another large village of the Hurons. This completed the disorganization of the tribe. They abandoned their villages and sought safety in different directions. A part of them, including all of the Tohotaenrat, made overtures to the Iroquois and were incorporated with the Senecas. Another party, after various wanderings, found their way to Orleans island, at Quebec, in 1651. In 1656 the Iroquois attacked them there and carried off nearly one hundred. The survivors then asked peace, and the majority were incorporated with the Mohawks and Onondagas, while the remainder, who preferred to remain with the French, were finally settled at Lorette (q. v.), near Quebec, where they still remain.

The greater part of the Hurons had fled to the Tionontatis, who in their turn were attacked by the Iroquois in December, 1649, and, after a short struggle, the two tribes abandoned their country and fled together to Manitoulin island in Lake Huron. In 1651 they removed to Mackinaw island, at the outlet of Lake Michigan. Being still pursued by the Iroquois, they again removed about 1660 to the Noquet islands, at the mouth of Green bay of Lake Michigan. From this point they made their way down the Wisconsin river to the Mississippi, where they entered into friendly terms with the Illinois, but in consequence of the hostility of the Sioux ·they again returned to the mouth of Green bay. · At this time the band numbered about 500 souls, and there were probably others scattered among neighboring tribes. They soon afterward joined the Ottawas at Shaugawaumikong (La Pointe, Wis.), near the west end of Lake Superior, and

**Wyandot.**—*Continued.*

here, in 1665, Allouez founded the mission of Sainte Esprit. About 1670, again in consequence of the hostility of the Sioux, the place was abandoned, the Ottawas going to Manitoulin island, while the Hurons returned to Mackinaw, where they numbered about 500 in 1677. Some Ottawas settled near them in another village, and the mission of St. Ignace was established among them under Marquette. In 1702 the Hurons removed to Detroit in lower Michigan, leaving the Ottawas at Mackinaw. In 1723, under the name of Necariages, they were formally received by the Iroquois as the seventh nation of the confederacy, but this alliance was brought about through the negotiations of the English and never had any practical result. In 1728 the mission of Assumption was established among the Hurons at Detroit. In 1751 a part of them removed to a new village at Sandusky, Ohio. About this time they began to be known as Wyandots, and all distinction between Hurons and Tionontatis was lost. As those killed and incapacitated by the Iroquois during and after the final war were chiefly Hurons, while the Tionontatis had fled almost at the first attack, it seems probable that the modern Wyandots were mainly from the latter tribe. That those who fled west in 1650 were but a small part of the Hurons then existing is shown by the fact that in 1656 those among the Senecas were so numerous as to form a distinct village of their own, while in 1653 Le Moyne found 1000 among the Onondagas. In 1656, also, the Mohawks carried off nearly 100 of the Hurons, then near Quebec; while soon after the majority of that party joined the Iroquois, and the descendants of those who remained near Quebec still number nearly 300, considerably more than the whole number of Wyandots now in Indian Territory.

After settling at Detroit and Sandusky, the Wyandots spread along the whole southern and western shore of Lake Erie and gradually acquired a paramount influence among the tribes of the Ohio valley and lake region, so that, although one of the smallest tribes in point of numbers, they exercised the right to light the council fire at all general gatherings. They claimed authority over the greater part of Ohio, and the settlement of the Shawnees and Delawares in that region was effected by their permission. They took a prominent part in all the Indian movements in the Ohio region down to the close of the war of 1812, taking sides with the French until the close of Pontiac's war, and afterward supporting the British against the Americans. After the treaty of peace in 1815 they were confirmed in the possession of a large territory in Ohio and Michigan, most of which, however, they sold in 1818, reserving only a portion near Upper Sandusky, Ohio, and a smaller tract on Huron river, near Detroit, Michigan. These were sold in 1842 and the tribe removed to Kansas, where they settled on a tract between the Missouri and Kansas rivers, the present Wyandotte county. In 1855 they were declared citizens, but the result was so unsatisfactory that in 1867 their tribal organization was restored and they were removed to a small tract in the northeastern corner of the Indian Territory, where they now are.

The population of the Wyandots has been variously estimated, but with them, as with other tribes, the lowest estimates are generally most reliable. Their former importance as a tribe was altogether disproportionate to their numbers, and in 1794 it was said that they never had more than 150 warriors in battle. The old estimates of Huron population have been previously noted, and from 1650 down to their settlement at Detroit they seem never to have had more than about 500 in one body. Later estimates are 1000, with 300 more at Lorette (1736); 500 (1748); 850 (1748); 1250 (1765); 1500 (1794–95); 1000 (1812); 1250 (1812). Only the first of these estimates includes the "Hurons of Lorette," Quebec, who were estimated at 300 in 1736, and were officially reported in 1900 at 448. They have a large admixture of white blood. There is another band known as "Wyandottes of Anderdon" in Essex county, Ontario, which numbered 98 in 1884, but these are now reduced to about half a dozen, the remainder possibly having joined their kindred at Lorette. Those in the Indian Territory numbered 251 in 1885 and 342 in 1901, making the whole number of Wyandots, or Hurons, now officially known in the United States and Canada about 800. Those in the Indian Territory have hardly a full-blood among them. There are probably a few in Kansas, who left the main body in

# DICTIONARY OF INDIANS.

**Wyandot.**—*Continued.*
1855, when tribal relations were for a short 'time abolished. For their villages, see IROQUOIAN.
There is some confusion in regard to the Wyandot gentes. From all that can be learned there seems to be no doubt that the three divisions of the old Hurons, above mentioned, were either gentes or phratries. Of these the Bear nation held the principal place, and at the Maumee conference in 1793 the Bear was the totem affixed to the signature of the Wyandots. In 1736 Chauvignerie gave their totems as the Turtle, Beaver, and Plover, while in 1761 Jefferys gave them as the Bear or Roebuck, Wolf, and Tortoise, while he states their tribal totem to be the Porcupine. The Tionontati gentes were probably added to those of the Hurons after 1650. According to Powell (Abst. Trans. Anth. Soc. Wash, pp. 77-8, 1881) the Wyandots, at the time of leaving Ohio, had eleven gentes, viz.: Deer, Bear, Highland Turtle (striped), Highland Turtle (black), Mud Turtle, Smooth Large Turtle, Hawk, Beaver, Wolf, Sea Snake, and Porcupine. This agrees with Morgan's list, excepting that Morgan's Turtle gens is here sub-divided into four gentes. These eleven gentes are arranged in four phratries, each having three gentes in the order given above, excepting the last, which has but two. According to Morgan (Anc. Soc., 153, 1877), they have eight gentes, as follows:

1, Ah-na-resé-kwä, bone gnawers (wolf). 2, Ah-nu-yeh', tree liver (bear). 3, Tso-tä'-ee, shy animal (beaver). 4, Geah'-wich, fine land (turtle). 5, Os-ken'-o-toh, roaming (deer). 6, Sine-gain-see, creeping (snake). 7, Ya-ra-hats-see, tall tree (porcupine). 8, Dä-soak, flying (hawk).

For further information see Powell, Wyandot Government, First Rep. Bur. Eth., 1879-80. (J.M.)

---

**Ahouandate.**—Schoolcraft, Ind. Tribes, III, 522, 1853.
**Ahwändate.**—Featherstonhaugh, Canoe Voy., I, 108, 1847.
**Anigh Kalicken.**—Post (1758) in Proud, Pa., II, 113, 1798. (Another form of Necariaga.)
**Bons Irocois.**—Champlain (1603), Œuv., II, 47, 1870.
**Charioquois.**—Ibid. (1611), III, 244. (Probably from the name of a chief.)
**Delamattanoes.**—Post, op. cit., app. 120.
**Delamattenoos.**—Loskiel (1794) in Kauffman, West Pa., app., 355, 1851.
**Delemattanoes.**—Post (1758) in ibid., app. 118.
**Dellamattanoes.**—Barton, New Views, app., 8, 1798. (Delaware name.)
**Ennikaragi.**—Lamberville (1686) in N. Y. Doc. Col. Hist., III, 489, 1853. (The editor thinks them the Ottawas.)
**Euyrons.**—Van der Donck (1656) in N. Y. Hist. Soc. Coll., 2d ser., I, 209, 1841.
**Guyandot.**—Parkman, Pioneers, xxiv, 1883.
**Gyandottes.**—Gallatin in Trans. Am. Eth. Soc, II, 103, 1848.
**Harones.**—Rasle translation (1724) in Mass. Hist. Soc. Coll., 2d s., II, 246, 1814.
**Hiroons.**—Gorges (1658) in Maine Hist. Soc. Coll., II, 67, 1847.
**Houandates.**—Sagard (1632), Can. (Dict.), IV, 1866.
**Hounondate.**—Coxe, Carolana, 44, 1741.
**Hourons.**—Tonti (1682) in French, Hist. Coll. La., 169, 1846.
**Huron.**—Jesuit Relations, 14, 1632.
**Hurones.**—Vaillant (1688) in N. Y. Doc. Col. Hist., III, 524, 1853.
**Huronnes.**—Hildreth, Pioneer Hist., 9, 1848.
**hurrons.**—Writer of 1761 in Mass. Hist. Soc. Coll., 4th s., IX, 427-8, 1871.
**Lamatan.**—Rafinesque, Am. Nations, I, 139, 1836. (Delaware name.)
**lemikariagi.**—Lamberville (1686, transl.) in N. Y. Doc. Col. Hist., III, 489, 1853.
**Little Mingoes.**—Pownall, map of N. Am., app., 8, 1776.
**Menchon.**—Duro, Don Diego de Peñalosa, 43, 1882.
**Nadowa.**—For forms of this name applied to the Wyandots, see *Nadowa.*
**Necaragee.**—Douglass, Summary, I, 181, 1755.
**Necariages.**—Gale, Upper Miss., 160, 1867.
**Negheariages.**—Document of 1723 in N. Y. Doc. Col. Hist., V, 695, 1855.
**Neghkareage.**—Albany conference (1723) in ibid., 693. (Given as the name of two of the six "castles" of the "Denighcariages" near Michilimackinac.)
**Neghkereages.**—Colden (1727) in ibid., III, 489, 1853.
**Nehkereages.**—Colden (1727), Five Nat., 21, 1747.
**Nicariages.**—Lattré, U. S. Map, 1784.
**Nicariagua.**—Clark, Onondaga, I, 306, 1849.
**Nickariageys.**—Canajoharie conference (1759) in N. Y. Doc. Col. Hist., VII, 384, 1856.
**Ochasteguin.**—Champlain (1609), Œuv., III, 176, 1870. (From name of chief.)
**Ochatagin.**—Ibid., 219.
**Ochataiguin.**—Ibid., 174.
**Ochategin.**—Ibid. (1632), V, 1st pt., 177.
**Ochateguin.**—Ibid. (1609), III, 175.
**Ochatequins.**—Ibid., 198.
**Ouaouakecinatouek.**—Potier in Parkman, Pioneers, xxiv, 1883.
**Ouendat.**—Jesuit Relations, 35, 1640.
**Owandats.**—Weiser (1748) in Kauffman, West. Pa., app. 16, 1851.
**Owendaets.**—Peters (1750) in N. Y. Doc. Col. Hist., VI, 596, 1855.
**Owendats.**—Croghan (1750) in Kauffman, West. Pa., app. 26, 1851.
**Owendot.**—Hamilton (1760) in Mass. Hist. Soc. Coll., 4th s., IX, 279, 1871.
**Quatoges.**—Albany conference (1726) in N. Y. Doc. Col. Hist., V, 791, 1855.
**Quatoghees.**—Note in N. Y. Doc. Col. Hist., VI, 391, 1855.
**Quatoghies.**—Garangula (1684) in Williams, Vermont, I, 504, 1809.
**Sastaghretsy.**—Post (1758) in Proud, Pa., II, app., 113, 1798.
**Sastharhetsi.**—La Potherie, Hist. Am. Sept., III, 223, 1753. (Iroquois name.)
**Talaman.**—Walam Olum (1833) in Brinton, Lenape Leg., 200, 1885.
**Talamatun.**—Squier in Beach, Ind. Miscel., 28, 1877.
**Telamaenon.**—Hewitt after Journeycake, a Delaware. ("Coming out of a mountain or cave"; Delaware name.)
**Telematinos.**—Document of 1759, in Brinton, Lenape Leg., 231, 1885.